"I will give you... the valley of Achor for a door of hope...:   *Hosea 2:15*

Achor. lit. valley of Trouble. ref. Joshua 7:24-26, the place where God judged Israel's sin

The Door of Hope

Stanley Voke

RIGHTEOUS BOOKS PUBLISHING
OTLEY, ENGLAND

THE DOOR OF HOPE

published by Righteous Books
First Floor, Century Buildings, 48-52 Westgate
Otley, West Yorkshire, LS21 3AS
England
Fax: 01943 850092
www.righteousbooks.com

©1998 Righteous Books

All Rights Reserved.
No part of this publication may be reproduced, stored in a retrieval system,
or transmitted in any form or by any means - printed, photocopied, electronic,
recorded, mechanical or otherwise - without prior written permission of the publisher.

International Standard Book Number: 1-900662-01-9

Most scripture quotations, unless otherwise indicated, are taken from the
HOLY BIBLE, NEW INTERNATIONAL VERSION®. NIV®.
Copyright ©1973, 1978, 1984 by International Bible Society.
Used by permission of Zondervan Publishing House.
All Rights Reserved.

Also used is the King James Bible, referenced as 'AV'.

•

Cover Design: Steve Aspinall, Image Design (Otley)
Typesetting & Layout: Image Design (Otley)

U.S.A. Distributors and Agents for Righteous Books:
Living Proof Inc.
PO Box 637, Bishop, California 93515

Printed in the United Kingdom by Creative Print & Design Wales, Ebbw Vale.

Contents

Introduction by Rev. Jim Graham 7
Foreword by Wayne Taylor 11
Preface to The Door of Hope 13

1	The Tip	15
2	Back to the Cross	21
3	Center Point	29
4	The Place Called Calvary	37
5	The Clenched Fist	45
6	Who Takes The Blame?	53
7	Reconciliation	59
8	God on our Side	69
9	Unfailing Love	77
10	The Cross in the Heart of God	89
11	The Cross in the Life of Jesus	97
12	The Cross and Salvation	107
13	The Cross and the Self-Life	115
14	The Cross and the Church	123
15	The Servant Heart	131
16	Where is the Lamb?	137
17	The Victory of the Lamb	143
18	The Final Breakthrough	149

Introduction
by Rev. Jim Graham

Stanley Voke wrote in his book 'Reality':

"My idea of revival had always been of some spiritual flood that would somehow, some day, come from God. I had no thought of the Streams that might cause it until one day I met a man from Africa who had been in a revival. He came at a time when, barren in my ministry and defeated in my life, I longed for God to revive the Church, yet laid the blame for lack of blessing on everyone except myself.
It was his simple testimony that impressed me. He claimed only to be a needy sinner, yet his face shone with peace and joy as he spoke of the Lord Jesus and the power of His precious blood to cleanse day by day. Soon God began to convict me, causing me to repent of one thing after another until my wife and I together with others in the church found ourselves walking a new path of penitence and fellowship, hesitatingly at first, sometimes even unwillingly. But God faithfully showed us where and how we needed to come back again and again to the Cross. The streams of Grace had begun to flow..."

There were five keynotes in Stanley Voke's life and ministry.

i. The Need for Repentance
This was no cosmetic, emotional, superficial expression of regret. This intruded into the deep places of his being. Sin had to be recognised and identified by his head as sin - not excused, justified, or ignored as shortcoming or weakness or the natural frailty of our humanity.
Sin, thus recognised, had to be felt in the heart for what it is. In other words sorrow for that sin was to be the sorrow God feels about sin.
Sin had to be confessed with the mouth before God and others and turned from by an act of the will. Repentance operated in the area of decision, not simply in the area of emotion. Where it was possible and appropriate sin required that restitution was made for it.
Repentance was never seen to be repressive, or negative or destructive, but rather it was liberating and positive and creative. Basilea Schlink has titled one of her books 'Repentance - the Joy-filled Life.' So it was for Stanley Voke.

ii. The Abundance of God's Grace

Grace is the sheer undeserved generosity of God's heart. Again he wrote in 'Reality'
"This is the paradox of Grace. He who insists he is right will be pronounced wrong, while he who admits he is wrong will be declared right."
For Stanley Voke grace was always "God's attitude to sinners by which He does for them what they do not deserve and in them what they cannot achieve."
Dr. F.B. Meyer, the great expositor and teacher of a past generation once said,
"I used to think God's gifts were in shelves one above another, and the taller we grow in Christian character the easier we could reach them. I now find that God's gifts are on shelves one beneath the other. It is not a question of growing taller, but stooping lower. We have to go down, always down, to get the best gifts."
So we can sing!

> *Marvellous Grace of our loving Lord;*
> *Grace that exceeds our sin and guilt.*
> *Yonder on Calvary's mount outpoured;*
> *There where the blood of the Lamb was spilt.*
>
> *Grace, Grace, God's Grace,*
> *Grace that will pardon and cleanse within.*
> *Grace, Grace, God's Grace,*
> *Grace that is greater than all our sin*

iii. The Overwhelming Wonder of the Cross

The Holy Spirit never comes to condemn us, but he does come to convict us and then lead us to Jesus and Calvary for cleansing and forgiveness and freedom. Constantly there is a 'fountain open for sin and uncleanness.'
It is at the Cross that death is defeated, righteousness is satisfied, sin is forgiven, full salvation flows (again), God is revealed, evil is defeated, freedom is given to live a righteous life, fellowship is real, selfishness is challenged, prayer is effective, hope is eternal, heaven is opened, servanthood is triumphant, the Holy Spirit is released, wholeness becomes possible, and God's peace is a reality.
No wonder Stanley Voke constantly raised the Cross of Jesus before the eyes and hearts of penitent men and women.

iv. The Reality of the Transforming Power of the Holy Spirit

From the very beginning but increasingly as the years passed Stanley had a greater openness to the person and the ministry of the Holy Spirit. He had a great yearning for all that God wanted to give. That might mean that he would be 'labelled' by evangelical brethren and others - so be it!!

What Jesus had made possible on the Cross the Holy Spirit wanted to make more powerfully and practically actual in our lives. There is a rich and real spiritual geography to be discovered and explored beyond the Cross. Good Friday came before Pentecost in history, but also in experience.

What God did for me at Calvary, He wants to do in me by His gracious Spirit.

v. The Anticipation of Being With Jesus Forever

Death was never the end, but simply a new beginning. It was not only an exit, but also an entrance. It does not take us into the darkness of the night, but into the dawning of a new day that never ends. It is departure, but it is also homecoming, so inevitably it can never be regarded as tragedy, but rather as triumph.

In heaven there is service without weariness, life without death, joy without sorrow, light without darkness, glory without suffering, satisfaction without want, beauty without infirmity, living without sinning, and presence without absence. Who could possibly shrink from leaving the land of the dying and going to the land of the living?

I thank God for the life and ministry of Stanley Voke. It has impacted my life at its deepest and most lasting level. To God be the glory for such a life.

Rev. Jim Graham,
Gold Hill Baptist Church,
Chalfont St Peter, Buckinghamshire

Foreword
by Wayne Taylor

'The Door of Hope' by Stanley Voke may be the most inspiring and practical book on the Cross written in recent time. As I read it, every page drew me nearer to my Saviour's side. The opening chapter on 'The Tip' or 'the dump' as we call it in America, is a masterpiece of illustration describing how Jesus' Cross disposes of all our "garbage," and lightens us of our load. I could hear my dear friend Stanley's voice telling that story as I read along. As always it was refreshingly convicting and captivating at the same time. This is the case with 'The Door of Hope' from cover to cover. The Cross of our Lord comes to life for the reader with fresh, piercing insight that transforms the heart. And the lasting lessons are that repentance leads to rejoicing, that coming to the Cross deepens spiritual communion, and that the way of brokenness is the way of blessing. As Stanley Voke says in 'The Door of Hope,' *"What we call 'brokenness' is not simply going occasionally to the Cross, but learning to live there... this is the only true way of peace and blessing."*

Stanley Voke was a friend of mine for many years and a blessing from Heaven to all of the Calvary Chapel Pastors in the North West of America. Without exaggeration he was one of the most influential mentors we had in the last several years. We had the wonderful privilege of 'sitting at his feet' at meetings and conferences, listening to his insightful message of Grace and repentance, the Lamb, and the Cross, while our hearts were melted and transformed because of it. Stanley's wit and warmth adorned his ministry and message so well, he was a joy to listen to and be around. His ministry was filled with the Word and the Holy Spirit, he himself exuded God's love for people. He was a man of deep devotion to God's Word, he was passionate in his love for Jesus Christ. 'The Door of Hope' is a book that embraces and expresses in delightful style Stanley's inspired appreciation of the finished work of Calvary.

Wayne Taylor,
Pastor, Calvary Fellowship, Seattle.

Preface

How many bruised, bewildered and sometimes despairing people there are in the world today - some of them in the churches. They are looking for a "door of hope" which might lead them through to a new kind of life, yet not knowing where to look. There is such a door which leads to forgiveness, peace and eternal life. It is the Cross of Christ.

In this book you will read of some of the different aspects of Christ's death which, as well as being the foundation of our Christian life, are vital in our day to day experience. I have tried to put these profound truths in simple language while basing everything on Scripture using mainly the New International Version. To write about the mystery of the atonement is a humbling experience because words are inadequate, but these are truths which must be shared. Whilst you may wish to read the book right through, we suggest you take one chapter at a time for your personal reading or for group Bible study.

Doreen, my wife, has spent many hours working with me over each chapter. She assures me she has enjoyed the task not least because we have been able to recall together those times when God led us into blessing by showing us again the grace of our Saviour in His death for us at Calvary. Our faithful friend Audrey Turner has typed the manuscript. I am so grateful to her.

In the days when I used to give children's talks I had a picture of a cross in the base of which was a little door. It was low and narrow, but it led to a bright pathway running through beautiful countryside. Coming to the door were people of all types and ages. They were leaving behind their cumbersome baggage and bending low to go through the door.

Our prayer is that many of you who read this book will join them. The door in the cross is still open for any who will repent of their sins and trust in the Lord Jesus who by His death and resurrection has opened for us all the Door of Hope.

Stanley Voke
Cobham, Surrey
1996

ONE | The Tip

Some years ago I retired from church pastoral work to join the noble order of "tramp preachers". This meant Doreen and I moved from a family-sized manse to a smaller house suitable for the two of us. What surprised us was the amount of stuff we had accumulated over the years. "Where had it all come from?" we asked ourselves and "Wherever can we put it?"

Now before we moved, our new home had been renovated and decorated. As a result, pieces of carpet, cardboard, plaster and wood, rubble of every kind - were piled up in the back garden. We gave what we could to the garbage man and then began to grow desperate. A local friend made a helpful suggestion. A mile or two away was a useful place where he had often taken his rubbish. It was a huge, fenced-in area known as "The Tip" or what our American friends call "The Dump." Anyone could take unwanted things there at any time.

So, cramming what we could into the back of our "hatch-back," we set off with our first load. Having never been there before we were a bit nervous, as well as uncertain of the way. But following the directions, we arrived to find great piles of stuff, everything from grass cuttings to old refrigerators. All around us were people carrying bags of waste material to hurl them on to the waiting mounds. Timidly we joined them, dumped our load and then followed the line of empty cars as they drove away. We began to feel exhilarated. I said to Doreen "Oh, I'm so glad to have got rid of all that stuff." She said, "So am I. You know, it's like going to the cross with our sin." We talked about this for a while and as we did so, we began to praise the Lord.

Outside the Camp

I remembered the words in Luke 23:33 - "When they were come to the place called Calvary." Those people came there literally. We have to come there in a spiritual sense as we repent of our wrongdoing and put our trust in the work God did at the cross. There He disposed of all our garbage of sin and guilt in the sacrifice of His Son. We saw how the cross was, dare we say it, the great "refuse tip" of all the world's wrong.

We had to go out of town to reach the Tip and remembered how the Israelites, when in the desert, had to go outside their camp to dump their refuse. It was a horrible place where, in addition to the garbage, lepers were taken to live in isolation, criminals were stoned to death and the unwanted bodies of sacrificial animals were burned.Like our Tip it was not at all a pleasant place. We are told in Hebrews chapter 13 that Jesus, in order to save us by His sacrifice, suffered "outside the camp." He went carrying His cross to the criminals' place beyond the wall of the holy city, Jerusalem, to the hill of execution where He was "made sin for us." There He took all our moral garbage so that we might be free.

But we must come to the cross as well, because there is no other place where our sin and guilt can be unloaded.

Goodbye to the Garbage

At the Tip we parted with things. Some of them gladly. They had been around too long. On to the mound we hurled them with relief. Others we left reluctantly. Was there no value in that cherished object? No place where it would fit? Would no-one buy it? Even take it for free? No! There was only one place for it - the Tip! Only one person who would take it - the man in charge of the Tip.

Many others must have felt as we did. We saw radios and refrigerators, cabinets and kitchen sinks, television sets and washing machines all lying around like so many fallen kings. We felt sorry for them, longed to reinstate them, but their days had gone and their glory passed away. Newer and better things had taken their place, indeed all were in some way defective. Once they had been gain. Now they were loss. Fit only for the Tip.

Praise God when we are glad to part with sin, to have done with all that spoils and offends our heavenly Father. When we see that Jesus has taken it in the judgement of the cross. Then we can come and judge it as well in repentance. But what of those long-loved habits and personal traits we regard as precious? Our indispensable idols? Our own righteousness? The apostle Paul faced the loss of these cherished things. In Philippians chapter 2 he made a list of all that was "gain" to him, giving him "confidence in the flesh" because, as he thought, they put him in credit with God. Such things as his ancestry, orthodoxy, religious zeal and culture - all so full of corrosive pride. When he came to know Jesus, however, everything changed. His "gains" became "losses" and his precious things "refuse" to be taken to God's Tip, the cross. Isaac Watts summed it up when he wrote:

> *When I survey the wondrous cross*
> *On which the prince of glory died;*
> *My richest gain I count but loss,*
> *And pour contempt on all my pride.*

All very well to sing it. But what happens when my will is crossed? My "ego" deflated? If I have to admit fault or take blame? If I am wrongly accused or my precious reputation is tarnished? Do I argue, get annoyed, defend myself or sink into self-pity? Or do I come to the place called Calvary and sacrifice to His blood "all the vain things that charm me most."? This means I may have to take to the cross not only what I know is vile, but what I regard as precious. Especially my own righteousness.

Lighter and Cleaner

Things were different for us as we left the Tip. The car was lighter and cleaner. So too were our spirits. The burden was gone. The bother was over. The clutter cast away. Everything was brighter. We drove away smiling. So, we noticed, did others, all glad to be free of their rubbish.

Why should we be afraid to come to the Cross? It is the place of liberation as it says in Ephesians 1:7 "We have redemption through His blood, the forgiveness of sins." What a glorious experience! Redemption! Freedom from bondage! We are loosed from guilt and fear and vain regrets. We need not struggle to let our garbage go. We can sing like Christian in 'Pilgrim's Progress' when he gave three leaps for joy at the foot of the cross and shouted,

> *What a place is this! Must here be the beginning of my bliss? Must here the burden fall from off my back? Blest Cross! Blest rather be the Man who was put to shame for me.*

We were surprised by the size of the Tip. Here was piled all the garbage of the district brought by an endless procession of cars and vans. Yet as fast as it came, it went, disposed of by the Refuse Department. Where it had gone we never knew. Nor did we care. No one ever saw again what they had brought to the Tip.

This made us think of the greatness of the cross and how mighty was the Son of God who died there. We read in Hebrews chapter 1 that He was the creator of the world, sustainer of all things and superior to angels and prophets. How mighty then was His sacrifice as He took on Him the sin of the world. Took it away to be destroyed in the fires of God's judgement. We need not fear to bring our little loads to the cross nor need we mourn over them any more. The grace of God is vastly greater than all our sin. The atoning blood of Christ is sufficient to satisfy all God's demands and enough to meet all our needs. We can be free to admit our failures and come to cast everything that offends Him down at the Cross.

We have to make more visits to the Tip. Garbage still gathers in our garden, but we do not let it stay there. Each journey is quicker than before. We have lost our fear and easily find the way. As we show in this book, we often have to go to the cross to repent of any known sin and receive fresh forgiveness. We do not have to travel far, but simply return to the Lord Jesus. What if we do not make this short journey? Then our garbage will pile up again. It will be like a house I knew which was neat and tidy on the outside, but inside was full of rubbish the owner kept picking up from the streets and storing. In the end it stank and the local health authorities had to be brought in to clean it out. If we are to be fit dwellings for the Holy Spirit, we need constantly to be made clean.

Common Ground at the Tip

There is a strange comradeship at the Tip. We do not know the others who come, but time after time we find one another doing the same thing in the same place - all bringing our garbage. We expect to see one another doing so. We say "Hello," smile, and part happy and free. Yet this is nothing compared with meeting one another at the spiritual Tip. There is no fellowship so real and liberating as that found at the cross. Karl Barth, the theologian, once said, 'When we recognise we are sinners, we perceive we are brothers." We are not exactly "brothers" at the local Tip, but we are at the spiritual one - the cross - where we are all known as sinners who repent and are made clean through the blood of Jesus. Here we are open and honest and made one in God's loving forgiveness.

We find cars of all kinds at the Tip. Saloons, vans, hatchbacks, trucks! Some are new and shiny, others old and even battered. One day we saw a man with a Rolls Royce! Whatever was he doing at the Tip?

We soon found out when he opened his boot [trunk]. In it he had the same kind of rubbish as we had in ours. So it is at the cross. Whoever we are, whether lofty or lowly, we have to come there with our sins, willing to have them uncovered and abandoned in repentance to the One who died because of them. Then we can be free. We are so glad there is a Tip. It was built long before we came and will still be there after we have gone, always available to meet the need of the whole community. No one need have garbage stacked in their yard if they are willing to go back whenever necessary to that place called the Tip.

TWO | **Back to the Cross**

Leo Tolstoy, in one of his writings describes three country scenes which he used as allegories. One of these tells how he came across some farm labourers trying to mend a cartwheel which had come to pieces. First they fixed the spokes into the rim of the wheel, then tried to force them into the hub. This didn't work, however, and after watching them struggle for a while he said, "Why don't you fasten the spokes into the hub first, then fix them one by one into the rim?" When they did this it worked perfectly. The point is that if we get things right at the center, those at the circumference will fit into place. If, however, the center is not in place, we only go on confused and frustrated.

The Center of Our Life

We need to ask ourselves what is the center of our life? What is it that in the final reckoning governs our personal objectives and activities? Is it self-interest or is it the will of God? How is it in the life of our church? We may spend our time occupied with things at the circumference. With plans and programmes, with forms of worship and minor doctrinal differences. With buildings and budgets and all the multifarious matters that keep us running around in a whirligig of activities. All of these we feel are necessary, and of course they do have their place. The trouble is they get into the center, dislodging what should be at the heart of the church. "The kingdom of God is not a matter of eating and drinking, but of righteousness, peace and joy in the Holy Spirit." [Romans 14: 17]

Christ's One Concern

The Lord Jesus Christ had a priority which governed His whole life. It was to do the will of God. That is why He came among us. He said "I came to do the will of Him who sent me." And in all the activities of His crowded life this was His one concern - to do what His Father commanded. There was however a focal point. You might think it was His birth or baptism, His lofty teaching or miracles, His prayer life or passion for the lost. All these were involved in doing the Father's will, yet they were only a preparation for His final sacrifice at Calvary by which He made atonement for the sins of the world. The Cross, which had always been in the mind of God, was also in the heart of Jesus. This is why He is called "The Lamb slain from the creation of the world." [Revelation 13:8] We shall see later something of what the cross means. For the present, suffice it to say it is not simply a carved object. Nor should we think only of the physical form of a dying man as we see on crucifixes. The cross is far more than this. It is the Son of God giving up His life through death as a sacrifice for sin. This is central to God's eternal purpose.

The Cross Displaced

In a book written some years ago by Archbishop George Carey, entitled "The Gate of Glory," he told of his concern at the way the cross seemed to be brushed aside today by certain Christians, when it is in fact the heart of our faith. It is the very gate of glory because it is the way through the barrier between man and God which sin has created. The cross must never be displaced. In recent times there have been a number of songs written about the triumph of Christ and the victory He makes possible in the christian life. With rousing music these songs are intended to express or stimulate joy. But sometimes when I have come to a service in spiritual need, even lacking any desire for worship, the triumphal emphasis at the beginning has only left me unmoved. Somehow I could not relate to it. But as soon as we sang a hymn about the cross I have found myself melted, even to tears as I saw again my Saviour's suffering love for me. Then I could worship at His feet as repentance came and gratitude flowed. Then I could enter into triumph, but it was the triumph of the Cross. This is not to say I do not appreciate songs about victory, glory or spiritual warfare. These are the fruits of revival and I love them. But why should they displace the cross in our worship? The same applies to conversation, testimony and preaching. How often do we talk to one another about the cross? Of the wonderful love of Jesus in dying for us, or of the forgiveness we are finding through the shedding of His precious blood? We hear testimonies about physical healings or unusual events which have happened in answer to prayer. All these are good and proper when truthfully recounted, but why so few testimonies about the joy of finding forgiveness and new life at Calvary?

A Different Testimony

I remember a testimony meeting when, one after another, people stood to share about all kinds of healings and helpings. The audience responded enthusiastically to each one with many a "Hallelujah!" Presently a sister stood and told how that morning she had lost her peace over a situation at home and had become resentful and angry with someone else. The Lord had helped her to repent and as she confessed her sin He had cleansed her, had filled her with peace and joy and restored her fellowship with the other person. Her face glowed as she spoke and she was full of praise. People were taken by surprise. There was a different quality about this testimony. It was on a deeper level because it touched on the moral issue of her sin and the broken relationship which Jesus had died to restore. In her testimony, Calvary had been brought into focus. And where the cross is central in our experience, repentance is inevitable, blessing is sure to follow and we can all say a heartfelt "Hallelujah!"

Sacrifice Central in Israel

One object was of supreme importance in the life of Israel. It was the Altar. There are at least five altars for sacrifice recorded in Genesis, the first was probably the one built by Abel, the next by Noah when he came out of the Ark. As for Abraham, he seems to have built one wherever he settled in his journeyings. Many years afterwards, when the nation had been saved from slavery in Egypt, a great bronze altar was built at the entrance to the Tabernacle and later the Temple of Solomon, governing both the approach and the worship of the people. Whoever came into the presence of God had to come first to the Altar. Later still when Ezra rebuilt the Temple after the return of the people from Babylon, before a single stone was laid they built an altar for sacrifices. It was the same with Elijah in his contest with the priests of Baal on Mount Carmel. (I Kings 18: 20-30) Before he prayed for the fire of God to fall, he first "repaired the altar of the Lord that was broken down." Do you see how basic to everything was the altar to which both people and nation had to come? There could be no forgiveness, no access, no worship, no fire from heaven, no glory of God's presence and no victory over the forces of evil without the altar and its offerings. The Altar in Israel is the Old Testament foreshadowing of the Cross on which Jesus the Lamb of God was to die for the sins of the world. This is dealt with more fully in the next chapter.

The Cross Central in the Church

I have mentioned that the cross was central in the purpose of God and in the mind and life of Christ. So it is throughout the New Testament, in the Gospels, the Epistles and the book of Revelation. Similarly in the life of the church the cross must be at the center, not as an object fixed on the front wall of a building or standing on the communion table, but as an experience in the life and work of the fellowship.

The first letter to the Corinthians was written by Paul to a church which had plenty of enthusiasm and spiritual gifts. It was also rich in knowledge and sound in doctrine and yet was struggling with problems which could have destroyed its life. In writing to help them, Paul says that when they first believed he had "resolved to know nothing while with them, except Jesus Christ and Him crucified." [1Corinthians 2:2] He taught the whole range of christian truth, but the cross was first and central. If you study First Corinthians carefully, as we shall do later in chapter 14 you will find that every problem among the members; division, disorder, immorality, marital trouble, lawsuits or charismatic confusion was dealt with in the light of the cross of Christ. In that light they could learn how to sacrifice, how to deal radically with moral issues, how to repent of rivalries and quarrels, how to humble themselves to one another, how to conduct their worship and above all how to practice "Calvary love" as described in 1 Corinthians 13. In writing to them it is as though Paul plants the cross in the center of the church, binding every issue back to Calvary. All this must apply to us as well.

Everything Comes from the Cross

Why is the Atonement so important? I believe because it is God's supreme act of grace and His great remedy for man's sin as we shall see later. That is why everything in Scripture and in the life of Christ leads to the cross and all that is in God's purpose flows from it. Jesus came into the world to die for sinners and were it not for Calvary there would be no salvation for any of us. No Saviour from sin, no way to the Father, no Holy Spirit here with us, no Christian life and no hope of heaven. Everything is made possible by the Cross.

An African Christian once had a vision of Jesus. He saw Him

bowed beneath a great load and asked, "Lord is that the sin of the world you are carrying?" The reply was, "No, it is your sin." At this the man was broken down in repentance, realising how lightly he had treated the load which weighed so heavily on his Saviour. I need to see Calvary like that. To see how great is my sin before God and how great was the judgment Jesus took for me. Then my hard heart is melted and my pride laid in the dust. All God's grace is made available to me as I repent - forgiveness, peace, acceptance with God, access into His presence, holiness, fellowship, victory over Satan and finally my very place in heaven. All because of what Christ has done for me. How then can we possibly evade or obscure the Cross?

On a car journey once, I found when halfway to my destination that I had left behind some important papers. There was nothing for it but to turn round and go all the way back. This was painful and humbling, but the only way on was to go back. Now, by nature I have always been very active and ambitious. My life could well be summed up in some words from Walter Scott's poem Marmion - "On, Stanley, On!" I was always striving to go on. On to greater achievements for God. Or so I thought! But there came a day when He said, "Back, Stanley, Back." I discovered that in all my ceaseless activities I had left the cross behind. My busy life was cluttered with all kinds of selfishness, yet like the people in Jeremiah's day [Jeremiah 8:6] I never stopped to repent. I was too busy to bow at Calvary. But I needed to go back there - to the place where I could look again on Jesus crucified for me, where in brokenness and repentance I might "wash and be clean." I often need to pray some lines of a Wesley hymn:

> *Coming as at first I came,*
> *To take and not bestow on Thee:*
> *Friend of sinners, spotless Lamb,*
> *Thy blood was shed for me.*

It is as though a voice calls to me again and again, "See from where you have fallen and repent." "Return to Me and I will return to you." I find that unless I am willing where necessary to go back in penitence, I cannot go on in peace. For spiritual revival and progress we need continual cleansing.

From Calvary to Pentecost

What applies to us personally must also apply to the church. I know of a Christian community which has the best of teaching, lively worship, plenty of spiritual gifts and a great vision to reach out to others. Yet at one time everything seemed to die. In distress they set aside a week of fasting and prayer to inquire into the cause of their decline. The Lord showed them various sins which had crept in among them unawares, such as mutual suspicions, envy, hardness of heart, pride and much else. As they repented of these things, wrongs were righted, relationships restored, the Holy Spirit started to work among them again and they began to "go on." In their next magazine their leader when writing about this said, "We thought we would go out in renewal from Pentecost. Instead we found we had to go back to Calvary."

God certainly wants us to go out from Pentecost, for without the power of the Holy Spirit we can do nothing. But first we must know the power of the cross. We need the blood of Jesus as well as the fire of the Spirit. Unless we live under the judgment of the cross so that we continually repent of sin and are made clean, we may well be found handling "false fire" and eventually no fire at all. If we are to go forward in the Spirit, we must be willing whenever necessary to go back to our centre-point - the Cross.

THREE | **Center Point**

When the Jews were travelling through the desert from Egypt to Canaan, they were told to build a simple structure of wood, curtains and skins, a tent in fact, erected as a worship centre. It was called the "Tabernacle" and you can read about it in the book of Exodus, one of the most extraordinary buildings ever constructed. I once saw a full-size model in Pennsylvania, USA. What surprised me was the large size of the bronze altar standing at the entrance. It was far bigger than any of the other pieces of furniture in the tent. When king Solomon replaced the Tabernacle with the Temple, [a grand and ornate building,] he made a huge altar with a surface of nine hundred square feet on which hundreds of sacrifices could be offered.

The Altar - Central in Israel

As we saw in the last chapter, Jewish life and worship were focused on the Altar where sacrifices were offered for sins. Without atoning sacrifices there could be neither forgiveness nor fellowship with God. Altars had existed from the very beginning since Abel brought his lamb for an offering, and later Noah built an altar after the flood. So it continued until centuries had passed and the people of Israel were brought out of Egypt. On the night of their liberation the all-important act was the killing of the passover lamb in every home. Then as they travelled through the desert their worship was centred on the Tabernacle in which were three altars. One was at the entrance, for sacrifices; another in the first room, for burning incense and in the inner room, called the Holiest, was the Mercy Seat. Here on the Day of

Atonement the blood of sacrifices was sprinkled in the presence of God for the sins of the whole nation. So you see from outside to inside an altar was there in one form or another to enable the people to have pardon, access and fellowship with God.

The altar was central for several reasons the first of which was atonement. This word means "covering" which was essential for sins to be removed from the sight of a Holy God, by the death of a sacrifice. This was the price which had to be paid for wrongdoing as God had told the people in Leviticus 17:11. The second reason was to provide a way to come to God. At the altar, forgiveness and reconciliation were made possible whenever they were needed. So throughout the years the way to God was kept open by continual recourse to altars where sinners confessed their sins, sacrifices were offered and God bestowed His mercy. In this manner both people and land were kept holy and God's judgments withheld as long as the altar with its all-important offering was in the centre. The altar was an awesome place where fires burned and blood flowed as men saw how their sinful behaviour caused their costly lambs to die. No one could come here lightly. No one went away unaffected. It was the place of judgment and yet the place of pardon.

The Cross - Central for Us

How is all this relevant today? And what should it mean to us personally? A great deal! Each altar in Israel pointed to the cross of Christ who was God's eternal Lamb and Calvary the earthly altar on which He died. His was the only effective offering for sin and all previous sacrifices were only valid as they foreshadowed His death. Just as the altar was central in Israel so the cross must be in our lives because it lies at the very heart of God's saving purposes. But, you ask, how must it be central? I believe first of all in our faith and teaching.

It was so for the apostle Paul who wrote to the Corinthians, "For what I received I passed on to you as of first importance: that

Christ died for our sins according to the Scriptures." [1Cor.15:3] And again as we saw in the last chapter, "When I came to you... I resolved to know nothing while I was with you except Jesus Christ and Him crucified." [1 Cor. 2:1-2] He taught them a great deal during his visits, but notice he says that "of first importance" was his teaching about the death of Christ. So also in all his letters the doctrine of the cross was basic to everything else and it must be the same with us.

Among the plants in my garden I once had a special one which was growing well until one day mysteriously it began to wither. I watered it, fed it and sprayed its leaves, all to no avail. It just went on fading away. So I dug it up to see what was wrong only to find that its main root had been damaged, probably through my own carelessness while digging nearby. The plant was not able to grow because its central source of life had ceased to function properly. It is the same with us. Our spiritual life and every truth in our faith comes from Christ through His atoning work on the cross. Get this out of place or become unclear about it and our Christian life will wither. It is essential then that the truth of the cross is clear in our doctrine.

The Cross in our Experience

What is more it must be central in our experience which grows from the root of our doctrine. What, I wonder, is the most important factor in your Christian experience? Is it prayer, vision, ecstasy, healing or miracles? Is it the filling of the Holy Spirit, Christian fellowship or service? All these are important and necessary, but surely since we are all sinners our basic and greatest need is for pardon. Without it we cannot be saved, we cannot know God nor enjoy any of His blessings. Forgiveness is His chief gift to us and His most costly. As it says in Ephesians 1:7 "We have redemption through His blood, the forgiveness of sins in accordance with the riches of God's grace." Notice that it comes to us solely through the blood of Christ shed for us on the cross where, by His death, He took all our guilt, alienation, and hostility towards God and one another. 'You who were far away have been brought near through the blood of Christ." "His purpose... was to reconcile both of them [that is Jew and Gentile] to God through the cross, by which He put to death their hostility." [Eph. 2: 13-16]

We all need forgiveness and reconciliation, and if we are to find these and live in them, it is only as we come to God's altar - the cross, then as we repent and come to the Lord for cleansing, we are able to forgive even as we are forgiven. It is as penitent sinners we come to Calvary where our sins appear in all their ugliness. Horatius Bonar wrote, *"He who would know holiness must understand sin, and he who would see sin as God sees it must look at the cross and know the meaning of Gethsemane and Golgotha."* An African Christian once said to me, "I never saw my sins until I saw them in the cross."

When we go easy on repentance it is usually because we have lost the sense of the holiness and love of God. If we avoid repentance, we evade the cross. If we love the one we will love the other.

The Cross in our Witness

The Cross must also be central in our preaching and witness. We are told by our Lord to "Go into all the world and proclaim the good news to all creation." [Mark 16:15] This is what the early Christians did. But what is this "good news"? It is the message of God's love in giving His Son to die for our sins. This is what people everywhere need to hear.

I remember a brother speaking once at an evangelistic event in which he gave glowing testimony of how he was "baptised in the Spirit." He then urged his hearers to seek and receive this wonderful blessing which was so real in his experience. What they first needed, however, was something more wonderful - forgiveness of their sins. This is the heart of our witness and we "short-change" the Gospel if we fail to share our own experience of forgiveness. It is no exaggeration to say that all effective evangelism springs from the experience of the cross. It was so when John Wesley "felt his heart strangely warmed" seeing, as he said, how "Christ had taken away my sins and saved me from the law of sin and death." From that point his great gospel ministry began. He was able to write:

> *Now I have found the ground wherein,*
> *Sure my soul's anchor may remain,*
> *The wounds of Jesus for my sin,*
> *Before the world's foundation slain.*

So it was with others. Bishop Festo Kivengeri of Uganda had a ministry filled with the love of God. It began one day when he says, "I saw, as if in a vision, Jesus hanging on the cross. I did not see just a helpless human being; I saw my God slaughtered for my sin. The death of Christ was because of me." Then came the message, "Now this is how much I love you." He was broken in repentance, then filled with the joy of forgiveness, the result of which was an intense longing to share the "good news" which he did throughout the world to the end of his life. Do we not all need to see the sacrifice of our Saviour in this personal way?

The Cross in our Worship

Finally the Cross must be central in our worship which should reflect the worship of heaven where it centres on "The Lamb on the Throne," the One "who had been slain." He is the sacrificed Lamb of God and in heaven He is praised and worshipped because of His redeeming blood.

> *Worthy the Lamb that died they cry,*
> *To be exalted thus,*
> *Worthy the Lamb our lips reply,*
> *For He was slain for us.*

Worship is real to me when I see Jesus, the Lamb on the Throne, the One who was sacrificed for me the sinner. As I look again on His wounds I am humbled and broken so that there pours from my heart adoration and love like the ointment that flowed from Mary's alabaster flask. [John 12:3.] After the Lord's resurrection, we read in Matthew 28:9 that 'When they saw Him, they worshipped Him." We continually need to see Jesus in our worship and always in the light of His death and risen life.

Changed Values

So, like Paul, we come to "boast in the Cross." [Galatians 6:14] How can we find any glory in such a scene of shame? Only as we see who it was who suffered there and what a tremendous work He did. The mighty and perfect Son of God took on Himself God's judgment against all our sins, putting them away for ever by His death. To men that death appears weak and foolish, but actually it is the wisdom and power of God dealing once and for all with the problem of human sin. [1 Cor. 1:18] What a difference when we see that in the cross God's justice was satisfied, forgiveness made possible, Satan's hold on us destroyed and new life made available to all who repent and believe. This is why Paul gloried in the cross. And so can we.

The Cross of Christ belongs to us. It was our sins He bore, our shame He took and it is His victory He gives us with all the benefits that flow from it. As we identify with Jesus in His death our values change. In the light of Calvary a door opens into the kingdom and glory of God. The cross alters everything for us - our condition before God, our relationship to Him, our priorities and our goals. Nothing we desire or possess, nothing we can achieve or take pride in on earth will in any way compare with that mighty, meaningful event in which lies all our hope - the death and resurrection of our Lord Jesus Christ. He was God's eternal Lamb who offered himself for us on God's great Altar! When we see this we can surely say with Isaac Watts:

> *Forbid it Lord that I should boast*
> *Save in the cross of Christ my God:*
> *All the vain things that charm me most,*
> *I sacrifice them to His blood.*

This will be possible only as we understand more of what the Cross meant for Jesus Himself.

FOUR | # The Place Called Calvary

When people visit the land of Israel they usually want to see the places connected with Jesus and His disciples, particularly the site of the crucifixion. Where this is, no one can be sure, but that there is such a place is clear from Biblical accounts, church tradition and historical records.

Calvary was a fearful place. Another name for it was Golgotha which means "Place of the Skull." One of the sites we saw when in Israel had a rock formation looking like a skull which may have given rise to the name. Be that as it may, the place where Jesus was crucified was horrible. Not all our sentimental singing about "a green hill far away" can ever soften the harsh realities of the blood and blasphemies, the shrieks and jeers which made a Roman execution of criminals such a ghastly affair. Calvary was a scene of torture where dying men lingered in agony under the gaze of pitiless eyes. Such was the place the Son of God accepted in which to end His earthly life.

The Fearful Frontier

Grim as these events are, it has been said that "the realities of the Hill of Shame are not so much physical as moral and spiritual." The Cross, fixed as it is in time has timeless significance. It was an event which God had purposed from all eternity, a fearful frontier Christ had to reach in order to save mankind. Here it was that men came with their hammers of hate and nails of unbelief, demanding the death of the Son of God, the One who had come to rescue them from their sins.

Some came to watch, some to wonder, others to weep, one at least to repent and find the door to Paradise. Long centuries before this, when the Jews sought to worship the Lord, He had said "There above the atonement cover over the ark, I will meet with you." [Exodus 25:22] This sacred object, which was kept in the Temple at Jerusalem, pointed to the cross of Calvary where we must all come in our spiritual experience if we are to meet with God.

The Cross has two aspects: In one we see Christ as our Redeemer by whom God made possible an atonement for sin, so that we could be freed from its guilt and its power over us. The other aspect shows us Christ as our Example, because the cross embodies certain principles by which every Christian is called to live. In this chapter we want to see what it meant for Jesus to die at the place called Calvary and discover how this must affect us, His followers.

The Lord of Glory

We have no conception of how great was the glory of Christ in His heavenly state. In His intimate prayer recorded in John chapter 17, Jesus spoke to God His Father of "the glory I had with you before the world began." [v.5] Later on in Colossians 1: 16-17 we read that "all things were created by Him and for Him. He is before all things and in Him all things hold together." We are also told in Hebrews 1:3 that He is "God's Son whom He appointed heir - [i.e. owner] of all things and through whom He made the universe. He is the radiance of God's glory and the exact representation of His being, sustaining all things by His powerful word." What a breath-taking description of Christ, Whether we think of "glory" as beauty, honour, power or moral perfection, Jesus had it all. He was the "Lord of Glory," loved by God the Father and worshipped by angels. Something of this was evident in His earthly life, even though it was "veiled" in His human flesh. John writes in his gospel that "We have seen His glory, the glory of the One and only who came from the Father, full of grace and truth." [John 1:14] This glory was shown physically to three of His disciples who, when with Him on a high mountain saw His whole appearance altered so that "His face shone like the sun" and "His clothes became as bright as a flash of lightning." {Matthew 17:2 Luke 9:29]

From Glory to Shame

This is the one who came to the Cross. The story is told in a passage in Philippians chapter 2 which may have been one of the first hymns sung by the early Christians. It describes Jesus who had the very nature of God taking one step after another, six in all, exchanging His glory for weakness, poverty, hardship and scorn until at the place called Calvary He hung helpless and stripped of everything. Nothing was more abhorrent to Him than evil, yet on the cross He was "made sin for us." He had laid aside His glory to be clothed with the filth of the world's wickedness. He who had a right to the adoration of angels did not "hide His face from mocking and spitting." [Isaiah 50:6]

One of the things we read men did to Jesus before taking Him to the cross was that they "spat in His face," one of the most degrading things that could be done to anyone. When we think how that face had shone like the sun in full splendour and still does, then we realise what depths of shame He plumbed so that sinners like you and me might share His glory. If anyone had a right to glory it was Jesus. He possessed all things. His was a glory by right as Son of God. Any glory we had, God gave us in our creation only to be spoiled by our sins. Even when we are saved from those sins and remade in new birth, the only glory we have is still what is given us. Yet how we seek our own glory! It is part of our original sin as it says in Romans 1:21, "Although they knew God they neither glorified Him as God nor gave Him thanks." We do not give glory to God if we are always seeking our own. How we hate to appear in the wrong, to lose face, reputation or our own righteousness. Yet on the cross this is exactly what happened to Jesus. Every shred of glory was stripped off and He was willing to be reckoned an object of contempt. In the light of this, how inappropriate is our self-glorying. I remember at one of our revival conferences I shared the platform with a brother, John, whose ministry had always been a blessing to me. I had given Bible teaching at two of the morning sessions and on the third when John was preaching I turned up on time to find the hall empty so I sat down, puzzled, and waited. Presently people began to arrive. The first said to me, "oh this is where you are. Didn't you know we were having a picture taken of the conference members and speakers?" I said I hadn't heard of it. "Oh," was the reply, "What a shame. Everyone else knew. We are all so sorry. Now you won't be in the picture." The meeting began. I didn't like the hymns. The worship didn't bless me and when John began to speak I thought, "He's not in good form this morning. What is the matter with him?" I was getting nothing from the "Word" and halfway through began to pray for John. The Lord said, "It's not John. It's you. You're in a pit because you were not in the picture. You are so used to being in the picture, in the centre of things, getting all the praise and glory and you don't like it when you are left out. You need to repent." I saw how full of resentment I was. How unwilling, even for once, not to be "in the picture." The Lord helped me to repent of my innate love of self-glory and to seek forgiveness. At once the message came alive. I began to praise the Lord and from then on to appreciate my brother's ministry.

Made Sin for us Sinners

Jesus was not only the Lord of Glory, but also the "Holy One of God." He was called this in the Old Testament, [Psalm 16:10] and by the angel who announced His birth, [Luke 1:35] then by demons whom He cast out, [Luke 4:34] by the apostles when preaching, [Acts 3:14] and again in Hebrews 7:26 and 1 John 2:20. The Holy One! Holiness is a profound quality. It means complete separation from all that is evil. In the Lord Jesus there was no alliance with sin, no taint of it even when He was tempted. To do wrong was hateful, repulsive, unthinkable to one who delighted only to do the will of God. He is called "Holy, harmless, undefiled, set apart from sinners, exalted above the heavens." [Heb. 7:26] Yet at the place called Calvary this "Holy One" hung before God and the world as One who was evil and vile. He was called "The Lamb of God who takes away the sin of the world," the One who "bore in His own body our sins on the Tree," who was "sent in the likeness of sinful man to be a sin offering." [John 1:29; 1 Peter 2:24; Rom 8:3] Profound statements describing the sufferings and death of our Lord. Yet none touch the heart of it like the words, "God made Him who had no sin to be sin for us so that in Him we might be made the righteousness of God." [2 Corinthians 5:21] He was made not only a sin offering but reckoned to be sin itself, becoming identified in the sight of God with all the evil of mankind. Here is a mystery we cannot fathom. We need to ponder this truth and try to realise something of what it must have meant for the Son of God to be "made sin" for us. Augustine once wrote, "He became what we were so that we might come where He is." In the light of this we must ask why, when He who was the Holy One of God was so willing to go to the Cross, we who are sinners so often refuse to go there? Calvary was what I might call "the sinner's place" where we need to come admitting what we are as we accept the conviction of God or the challenge of others. This is where we stand with bowed head and broken heart to admit we are wrong and repent. The sinner's place! The hardest place for any of us to take! And if we do take it, how quickly we leave it for some "higher" ground of our own righteousness. How different was Jesus.

> *He humbled himself to the manger,*
> *And even to Calvary's tree,*
> *But I am so proud and unwilling*
> *His humble disciple to be.*

Taking Our Condemnation

Jesus is also the final Judge of all men. He said He did not come into the world to judge but to save. But He also claimed that God the Father had committed all judgment to Him. We see this vividly in the book of Revelation where it is Jesus who administers the judgments of God as only He is fit to do. Yet at the Cross He who is the Judge of all allowed himself to be judged. "Take Him yourselves," said Pilate "and judge Him by your own law." [John 18:31] They did so, and unjustly condemned Him to a criminal's death. Yet in doing this men passed judgment on themselves. In nailing the Lord of Glory to the cross they were hammering home their own condemnation. At the same time God was judging all our pride and selfishness, our envy, hate and greed, our carnal wisdom and crafty politics which had conspired together in this dreadful act. We speak of the cross as the greatest evidence of God's love and so it was, but we must never forget it was also the clearest demonstration of His judgment. In the death of Christ God was judging our sins. That was the only way we could be forgiven.

> *Bearing shame and scoffing rude,*
> *In my place condemned He stood;*
> *Sealed my pardon with His blood;*
> *Hallelujah, what a Saviour!*

Now how does this affect our attitude to what is wrong in our own lives? Surely if God judged our sins in the cross, then we must judge them too, for we cannot condone what He has condemned. We cannot love what God hates or live accepting those things for which Christ died.

Repentance means we pass judgment on our own sins - every one however small, and we "take them to the cross" where they have already been judged. When I first saw this it meant I could no longer repent lightly and superficially. I had to see sin for the awful thing it is and condemn it. Once, when challenged by a friend about my jealous attitude, I shrugged it off saying, "A little bit of envy is nothing. Everyone is like that." He replied, "Brother, you may think it means nothing much, but for Jesus it meant the Cross. We are told it was for envy the chief priests handed Him over to Pilate." I have never forgotten his words and have since learned that every sin, however small, needs to be judged in the light of Calvary.

Dying Our Death

Here we touch the very depth of the Cross. It is natural that we mortals should die, but that He, the eternal Son of God, the giver of all life, should do so is indeed a mystery. Yet it was for this purpose He came into the world - to surrender Himself to death so that in being its victim He would become its victor. "The sting of death is sin," it says in 1 Corinthians 15:56, but as one writer puts it, "Death stung itself to death when it stung Christ." Death is the ultimate penalty for sin, not only physical death, but spiritual - fearful separation from God. Jesus suffered both on the Cross. He died for sin; died because of our sin. He also died to sin; died rather than sin! And in that death He took all our sin and cast it into oblivion so that neither it, nor the death it caused, could ever have any hold on Him. Nor on those who belong to Him.

In the death of Christ was the death of sin and the death of "self" in all its forms. As we look on the cross we see the Lord of life dying to His own glory, will, desires and comforts. Dying to the world's opinion of Him, to all resentment and recrimination even towards those who were crucifying Him. Dying to everything except the will of God His Father and His own undying love. And as we look on Him there, we see ourselves with all our selfishness nailed with Him to that cross. God has judged our sinful self in the judgment of Christ our substitute. Paul says much in his writings about this, how that he himself had been "crucified with Christ" and how "those who belong to Christ

Jesus have crucified the sinful nature with its passions and desires." [Gal.2:20. Rom.6:8. Gal.5:24]

Again he says, "Because one [i.e. Christ] died for all, therefore all died." That is to say, we died in Christ our representative. "And He died for all, that those who live should no longer live for themselves but for Him who died for them and was raised again." [2 Cor. 5: 14-15] At Calvary there was a mortal blow dealt at our self-life. We shall think about this again in Chapter 13.

Does this sound morbid and negative? By itself the cross may appear so, seeming incomplete, shrouded in darkness and despair. But we read in John 19:41 that "in the place where He was crucified there was a garden," a place where life sprang up and beauty flourished. Jesus died on the hill of shame, but in the garden nearby He rose again in victory. As we are willing to "die" on that hill, we too may rise to new life and power in our garden of resurrection.

This all sounds very good and we may be ready to accept its truth without knowing much about the experience of "dying to self." This has to be worked out each day in our attitude to God and to others as we let go what is selfish and allow the love of God to fill us. In the next chapter we shall consider what this means.

FIVE — The Clenched Fist

Dr. Joe Church, one of the pioneers in the East African revival, often used simple pictures to illustrate his talks. One of these showed a man drawn inside a capital letter "I." His neck is stiff, his face is angry and his fists clenched by his sides. He illustrates the hard unbroken man, full of pride and resentment. Another part of the picture showed the same man now in a letter "C" which begins the word "Christ." This time his head is bowed, his fists are unclenched, his hands cover his eyes, and with bent back he is on his knees. He is the same man, but he has come to the Cross. The picture represents the words of Galatians 2:20, "Not 'I' but 'Christ.'" We have all become used to seeing the clenched fist on our television screens. Communists used it as the symbol of their fight against capitalism. It was then adopted in African countries as the sign of their struggle against colonialism. Often we saw vast crowds of people punching the air with their fists as they shouted freedom slogans. The clenched fist which represented the reaction of people against oppression and injustice sadly became an expression of hatred and violence. We clench our fists from the time we are born. Even babies, crying because they are hungry or in pain, clench their tiny fists. We adults do the same when we are frustrated or angry. Fists indicate determination, hostility, rage and rebellion. They are what boxers use to knock out their opponents, and angry people to threaten others. Speakers clench their fists and bang the table to vent their irritation or drive home a point. Fists are not signs of gentleness, peace or mutual co-operation, but rather of tension, resistance and antagonism. The clenched fist also means that we grip and hold something for ourselves. It signifies a refusal to let go what we consider to be our right. We set ourselves against others and show our determination to have our own way by clenching our fists.

Does God Clench His Fists?

Can we ever say that God clenches His fists? Yes! For instance in the book of Proverbs chapter 30 verse 4 we read of Him "gathering the wind in His fists," which is a way of saying that He holds natural forces in His power. The teaching of Scripture shows that Nature is subject to the control of the Creator. It is not a law unto itself.

Many times in the Bible we read of the "hand of the Lord." Just as in human life we may use our hands either to serve others or to strike them, so the Scripture describes God's hand being either "upon" people to bless them or "against" them in judgment. God is said to "open" His hand so as to satisfy men with good things. [Psalms 104: 28 and 145: 16] He does not hold back any thing that is right for us as it says in Romans 8:32, "He who did not spare His own Son but gave Him up for us all, will He not also along with Him graciously give us all things." He is the God with the open hand, but also the one who clenches His fist in anger against evil and therefore towards all who refuse to be parted from their sins. In Judges 2:15 we read of the "hand of the Lord" even being against His own people because of their sinful idolatry, so that they were brought into great distress. To the wicked and impenitent, God must be the Judge with the closed fist. To those who turn to Him in repentance and faith He is the Father with the opened hand.

Do We Not Clench Our Fists?

This raises the serious issue that in one way or another we have all raised our fists against God. Not perhaps with our hands [although some people have] but in our hearts and attitudes. We are not simply lost sheep who have gone astray. We are rebels against God. Rebellion against authority was a capital offence in Israel, whether towards parents or civil rulers. We are guilty of the worst form of this offence - rebellion against our heavenly Father, the King of kings. We may not like to think we are, but we are shown up when we are unwilling to submit to God, hardening our hearts against His will and choosing to go our own way instead of His. That is why it says in Romans 8 verse 7 that "the sinful mind is hostile [at enmity] towards God. It does not submit to His law nor can it do so." Rebellion, as we show in chapter 11, was the original sin of Satan who lifted himself up against his Creator and tempted us to do the same. This attitude is evident throughout human history and is deeply rooted in each one of us. We resist the gentle pressure of the Lord and begin to clench that inner "fist" when we say "No" to Him over some issue or other. Such resistance is the root of rebellion. How often I have been guilty of having this attitude of hardness towards the Lord, only to lose my peace and joy until I return to Him and yield to His will. A man once complained that he had been through a "hard week" at home and at work. However he later confessed that the Lord had shown him it was not so much the week that was hard, but his own heart. That is why everything else had seemed hard. Perhaps you are going through some difficult situation. You feel that God does not care about you. There seems no answer to your prayers. You begin to question His goodness asking, "Why, Lord?" It is a natural response. The Scripture tells of people such as Job and Habakkuk, as well as David and other Psalmists, who asked this question at times. But if for any reason we come before the Lord with a "clenched fist" reaction, let us be ready not only to repent of it, but to open our hands in heartfelt prayer for pardon and fresh blessing. It is noticeable that the Jews always prayed lifting not clenched, but opened hands to God. [Exodus 9:29. 2 Chronicles 6:12,13]

Our Attitude Towards Others

So far we have been speaking of our attitude to God. But how about our relationship with other people? The symbol of the fist is often seen when one group of people react against their fellows. What frightful atrocities have been, and still are being committed throughout the world as men clench their fists against one another. But let us come nearer home. Do we not ourselves clench our fists towards others? Someone says or does something we do not like and we react with resentment. Our pride is hurt. Then bitterness begins to grow. This slowly hardens into anger and finally we want to strike out at those concerned or at anyone else who happens to cross our path. We may seem to be humble and pious, praying and worshipping with others, while under our friendly exterior we keep a clenched fist. We are like the people in Isaiah 58:4 of whom it was said, "Your fasting ends in quarrelling and strife and striking each other with wicked fists." It may not literally be so with us as it was with them. But within our thoughts and feelings a fight may be going on, which is just as serious in the sight of God. How we need to recognise these hidden fists and repent of them before they damage others as well as ourselves.

The Saviour with the Open Hands

What about Jesus? Did He have a clenched fist? There was enough around to rouse His anger and cause Him pain. Many times He spoke out against hypocrites, legalists, evildoers and those who desecrated the house of God. Jesus was never soft on sin. Nor should we ever be. But when He came into the world it was with open hands ready to seek and save lost men and women. Hands that were always open to God His Father in willing obedience and surrender. We are told in Philippians chapter 2 verses 6 and 7 that He "did not consider equality with God something to be grasped, but made himself nothing." He did not cling to glory, but took "the very nature of a servant." He stands in utter contrast to Satan who sought to strike at the Almighty with rebel fists, while Jesus the eternal Son of God submitted to His Father with surrendered hands. "Here I am," He says, "I have come to do your will, O God." [Hebrews 10:7] He came to us, and still comes, with open hands. In His earthly life Jesus used those hands to break bread for the hungry, bless little children, heal those who were ill or diseased and raise dead people to life. He was the open-handed servant of the Lord always reaching out towards others. Even when at last He was taken by His enemies, He refused to resist. When they struck Him He did not hit back, when they reviled Him He did not retaliate and when they laid Him on the cross He surrendered His open hands to the cruel nails, giving himself to bear in His body the sins of the world. Jesus died at Calvary not with clenched fists, but with hands still open both to God and man. "Shall I not drink the cup that my Father has given me?" He said. Even as the soldiers pierced His hands with the nails, He cried, "Father forgive them, they do not know what they are doing," and in final surrender to God He said, "Father into your hands I commit my spirit." [John 18:11. and Luke 23: 34 and 46] Jesus came to show that God has opened His hands to us in mercy and grace. The evidence is seen not only in the Saviour's life, but supremely in His atoning death on the cross.

When He rose again from the dead His hands were still open to bless and to give. We read in Luke 24:50 that after the resurrection, "When He had led the disciples out to the vicinity of Bethany, He lifted up His hands and blessed them. While He was blessing them He left them and was taken up into heaven." The last sight this world had of Jesus was of one with open hands outstretched towards us as He returned to His Father.

Closed Hands or Open Hearts?

Jesus came to us with open hands. But do we always approach others in the same way? We all too easily close our hearts in selfishness or hostility. In our garden we have some flowers called "African Daisies." When the sun is out they open their petals in bright sparkling colours. But as soon as darkness comes each flower closes up tightly and its beauty disappears. How like them I can be. When I am spiritually "in the dark" I become shut up in selfishness. It is only as I live in the light of the love of Jesus especially as seen in the Cross that I become open to reflect His beauty and reach out to others.

In South Africa, sadly, there has often been hostility between the Zulus and the Xosas. Many individuals from these tribes came to work in the mines around Johannesburg, where they lived in separate compounds. Unfortunately they brought their antagonisms with them so that at one time those living in one compound would never dare go into another and often there would be inter-tribal violence with terrible fighting and killing.

I have read how, on one occasion, a Zulu Christian, feeling that something must be done to put an end to this in his area, resolved to go into a Xosa compound and plead for reconciliation. When warned that he would probably be killed, he replied that, if need be, he was willing to die for the cause of peace. With great difficulty he gained entry to the hostile compound and was taken by the guards to the leader who was highly suspicious of him. When asked why he had come, the Christian first showed that he was unarmed and then said, "I have come to surrender myself to you." Such a thing was unheard of. After his initial shock, the Xosa leader surprised him by saying, "Well, if you have come here to surrender to me, then I must surrender to you." With this they clasped hands, embraced each other and eventually planned a council for peace in their compounds, which played a part in the movement of reconciliation leading up to the end of "apartheid." All because one man risked his own life and crossed into enemy territory to give himself up!

In this story we see what our Lord Jesus did. He came into enemy territory to surrender Himself into the hands of sinners so that He might die for those who hated Him. He came with empty hands!

With no weapon but perfect love so that He might reconcile us to God and to one another! As we face His cross what response can we make? We cannot stand there with clenched fists. If we do, we help to hammer the nails into His hands. We can only surrender to Him as He did to us. And in opening our hands and hearts to Him we must surely open them to one another.

We have seen that the clenched fist is a sign of anger and rebellion. But the Cross, the sign of the Christian faith, reminds us of the opened hands of the Son of God pierced for us, to pour out the lifeblood that brings forgiveness and reconciliation to all who believe.

We began this chapter with the picture of a man with a hard face and clenched fists standing in a letter "I." We then saw him with his body bowed in brokenness inside a letter "C." We can add one more piece to the picture, the same man standing again, but this time with shining face and open hands, reaching out in love and invitation.

How do you fit into this picture? Do you have a "clenched fist" attitude about anything, either towards God or someone else, say in your family, church or place of work? If so, this is the moment to repent, to seek forgiveness and a renewed relationship so that God can make you a person with open hands, sharing His blessing with others. To bow at the Cross means that your heart will be melted and your hands unclenched as you see Him who bowed His head and spread His hands for you on Calvary.

SIX | Who Takes The Blame?

The children's party is in full swing. Everyone is happy playing games until a few boys get rough, a table is knocked over and a vase crashes to the ground. Somebody asks, "Now who did that?" No reply. Then each one starts accusing someone else. No-one says, "It was my fault."

This is natural, you say. We hate to take the blame, so we try to place it elsewhere. We see the same throughout the world, in marriages, families, communities and between nations. One generation blames another for the ills of society. When last did you hear any politician accept blame? But how often have you heard one side put all the blame on the other? Quite regularly and quite recently! What tensions, hostilities, divisions and even wars, are caused because no-one will accept blame. So it goes on. From school playground to world arena the same cry is heard, "They started it. They are to blame." It is extraordinary what excuses we can make. Two young brothers were having a fight when the father intervened and said, "Here, what's all this about?" The older boy immediately said, "It's his fault. He hit me back!"

It Must Be God's Fault

Because this spirit of blaming is so common to us all, we are not surprised to find it everywhere in the Bible. Indeed it is there in the beginning when a man and a woman disobeyed God. They both tried to hide and when challenged about their wrongdoing, Adam blamed

Eve, she blamed the serpent and in the end Adam said, "The woman you put here with me - she gave me some fruit from the tree," implying that it was God's fault. [Genesis 3:12] We also read how, while Moses the spiritual leader was away receiving the Ten Commandments, Aaron the high priest of Israel made a gold image of a calf for the people to worship. It is true they had asked for the idol, but it was Aaron who actually carved it for them. Yet when Moses faced him with this great sin, he shifted his blame saying, "You know how prone these people are to evil. They said, 'Make us gods,' then they gave me the gold, I threw it into the fire and out came this calf!" [Exodus 32: 21-24] Can you imagine it? How foolish our excuses can be when we try to shift blame.

Later on Saul, the first king of Israel, disobeyed God on two occasions and when faced with his faults blamed Samuel the prophet in one case, and his soldiers in the other. [1 Samuel 13: 11-13 and 15: 17-19] The people of Israel were the same. During their journey to the promised land they continually grumbled, disobeyed God and rebelled against Him yet hardly ever accepted blame. It was either the fault of Moses for bringing them from Egypt, or it was "because of the way." We read, "they murmured against the Lord." [Numbers 21: 4,5.] He was to blame for everything. Do you see how serious is this blaming spirit?

Blaming All and Sundry

How like them we all are. When we do wrong we invariably look around for someone to blame, especially in our homes and families where we have to live closely together. Doreen and I spent years in our early married life scoring points off one another, always trying to put the other in the wrong about something. often it would be on trivial matters such as who spilled the milk or left the front door unlocked. It was like playing on a seesaw. Push your partner down and you push yourself up!

If it isn't people we blame, it is circumstances. If not the wife, then the weather! If not the children, then our "nerves" or our tiredness! We say, "I'm not really myself today. That's why I'm so snappy." I know because I've used all these excuses myself. Another way we place blame is to blame ourselves and hold on to our guilt. We say, "I can never forgive myself for doing that." The result is we live in self-pity and remorse, unwilling to accept ourselves as the people we really are and repent of our wrong action or attitude. Unwilling to forgive the person God forgives - myself.

In all these situations we are avoiding what we call "the sinner's place." Because of our pride we think that by blaming we gain something. We save face - preserve our reputation. The fact is however that we lose out disastrously. Adam lost Paradise. Aaron lost credibility. King Saul lost his kingdom and for forty years the Israelites lost their entry into the promised land. As for the thief who died on the cross cursing everyone, he lost heaven itself. And we, in avoiding blame, only add to our sin and forego the blessing of forgiveness. I have learned that blaming others and making excuses never covers my wrong. only the atoning blood of Jesus can do that. Let us all examine ourselves in this matter and ask, "When did I last willingly admit fault and accept blame, whether in my home, church or place of work? Am I better at placing blame on others than taking it myself?"

The Alternative - Taking Blame

In the Bible we find many, however, who took blame even when the fault lay with others. Daniel was one of the most blameless of men, but he prayed, "O Lord we have sinned and done wrong." Ezra was another such man and he prayed, "O God I am ashamed and disgraced to lift my face to you because of our sins." Nehemiah who was such an upright person prayed, "I confess the sins we, including myself, have committed." Notice how all these righteous men took blame along with the people. [Daniel 9:5; Ezra 9:6; Nehemiah 1: 6,7.]

Moses went even further. When the Israelites worshipped the golden calf Aaron had made, Moses pleaded with God saying, "oh what a great sin these people have committed. Please forgive them, but if not, then blot me out of your book." Exodus 32: 31 & 32.] He was willing to take the blame and even lose his place in God's kingdom, for the sake of the people. David was the same. In spite of the terrible things king Saul in his jealousy did to him, he never blamed him. Even when Saul massacred eighty- five priests who had given David a few loaves of bread when he and his men were starving, David said, "I am responsible." [1 Samuel 22:20] He was a man of humble and loving heart who would rather take the blame than put it on others.

Our Blame Taken at the Cross

All these men pointed to the Lord Jesus, the spotless Lamb of God, who came to take away our sin. In a world where we all accuse one another, He went to Calvary to take every vestige of our blame. There in the midst of the cursings, revilings and false accusations, to say nothing of the physical violence done to Him, His only response was, "Father forgive them for they do not know what they are doing." He bowed His head and accepted all our guilt so that He might one day, "present us holy and without blame in God's sight." [Colossians 1:22] Jesus by His death did a perfect work for those He died to save. As we see what our Saviour has done for us, we will at last understand that we can afford to take our own blame. We do not need to cover our faults or evade blame by putting it on others. Instead we can give both our sins and our blame to Christ in repentance and faith knowing that He has already taken them on the cross. Because Jesus bore all our wrong when He died, God is able to declare us right and we can be at peace. Being forgiven, we are then free to rebuke wrongdoing where we encounter it, and as we stand for justice and righteousness, challenge wrongdoers to take responsibility for their own actions so that they too may be willing to take their own blame.

However we shall not want to go around blaming others for every fault we see in them. Rather, as fellow sinners, we will take our place alongside them, sharing their blame in the same way that Moses and others were willing to do.

Johann S. Bach, the great musician, had a large family. One of his sons, Friedemann, greatly offended his father one day by telling him a lie and refusing to repent or ask forgiveness. As a result they were alienated. However his stepmother Magdalena, whom Johann loved very much, persuaded Friedemann with great difficulty to come with her to see his father. They went into his room and speaking first she said, "Father, we have come to say we are sorry." Melted to tears the boy repented and the father was reconciled. All because Magdalena had been willing to share the blame.

Pardon and Peace at the Cross

The Lord Jesus took all our blame. Then why should we go about putting it on others? If we do, we are on different ground from the Saviour. But if in any situation of fault we come to the sinner's place at the foot of the Cross, each one taking his own blame, then we find pardon and peace. As we do this in our homes and churches we discover one another at the Cross where tension and strife are taken away and love prevails.

What if we take blame, but the other one will not? What can we do then? The answer is to go on taking blame as Jesus did. Here is a testimony sent me by a lady who was in a church where I had preached. She wrote, "After you had spoken about being broken before the Lord, I was aware of a resentment I held in my heart against a brother in the church. I went to apologise to him and ask his forgiveness thinking 'This is brokenness.' He did not receive me in love, but instead accused me of much more than I was really guilty of. In fact he was quite horrid to me. Then the Holy Spirit showed me that true brokenness was knowing how Jesus reacted. When He was reviled, He did not revile again. How like Him to show me this and take me deeper into brokenness. How I praise Him. This is what He is after."

What we call "brokenness" is not simply going occasionally to the Cross, but learning to live there, willing to accept blame as Jesus did and letting God take care both of our reputation and our vindication. This is the only true way of peace and blessing. Who among us is willing to take blame so that we may never hinder reconciliation?

SEVEN | Reconciliation

Once while travelling in Kenya, Doreen and I drove for about a hundred miles down the Great Rift Valley stretching for thousands of miles from Tanzania to Jordan. All around us, trees, plants and flowers had carpeted the scene with beauty, yet beneath this covering the great rift was still there. As we looked around we thought of our human story. The Bible tells us that mankind became alienated from God at the very beginning of history and in spite of our covering of civilization and culture, the great spiritual rift remains. As the prophet Isaiah says, "Your sins have separated between you and your God." [Isa. 59:2]

There are some very deep valleys on the surface of the earth such as the Grand Canyon in the USA. But none can compare with the separation that exists between us and God - a canyon as deep as sin and as low as hell itself. We can only measure how serious it is by what it cost God to bridge it. The price of reconciliation was nothing less than the sacrifice of His own Son, the Lord Jesus Christ. In this chapter we consider the power of the Cross to reconcile us to God and to one another. The spiritual breach between us and God was caused by sin, which increased until people everywhere became filled with such corruption and violence that God had to send a great flood to destroy them. [See Gen. 6:5-7]

Yet even though He had to judge people so severely He gave the sign of the rainbow showing that He would not give up His purpose to restore and reconcile the world He had created. [Gen. 9:13] To bring this about God had to deal with sin.

The Sin of Rebellion

Sin is so serious that there are some twenty different words to describe it in the original languages of the Old and New Testaments covering every aspect of wrongdoing. Among them is the word "transgression" which occurs over a hundred times and is the strongest of them all because it also means "revolt" or "rebellion." We may sometimes trespass on someone's property without realising it. With no intention of violating their rights we just wander on to forbidden ground. On the other hand we may trespass deliberately, even continually, a far more serious situation. It is an act of rebellion against authority which is what the word "transgression" often means. Rebellion was the most serious offence in Israel. Rebellious sons could be stoned to death under the Mosaic law. Rebellion against the king also called for the death penalty. To rebel against the Lord, the "Most High" was the worst of all, bringing severe judgment on both land and people as we are told in Psalm 107 verses 10-12. In Isaiah chapter 1: 2-7 we see God mourning over the rebellion of His own children, "I reared children and brought them up, but they have rebelled against me." "They have forsaken the Lord ....and turned their backs on Him." Fearful results are then seen to follow. "Your country is desolate, your cities burned with fire, laid waste as when overthrown by strangers." Years before, when Saul the first king of Israel deliberately disobeyed the Lord by rejecting His precise orders in the war with the Amalekites, the prophet Samuel rebuked him with the words, "Rebellion is like the sin of divination and arrogance like the evil of idolatry. The Lord has rejected you as king." [1 Samuel 15:23]

The Results of Rebellion

Another example of rebellion and its dire results is seen in Absalom, King David's favourite son. A handsome and vain young prince, he made himself popular with his father's subjects, especially any who were on their way to the king with a complaint. He promised all kinds of reforms if he were king and in this way "stole the hearts" of the people from their loyalty to David. In spite of his father's forbearance he persisted in his conduct and eventually raised a revolt which led to a civil war. He had committed a double rebellion, not only against his father, but also against his king who had in every way sought reconciliation. Absalom however showed no sign of repentance or willingness to be reconciled. As a result he perished along with many others in the war that followed.

In this he points back to one described in Isaiah 14 and Ezekiel 28 as Lucifer, the guardian angel who was corrupted because of his beauty, then reached to take God's throne and was cast down to the earth to become Satan and work havoc in the human race. I describe this more fully in chapter 11.

The result of rebellion is twofold. On the one hand from God's side there is anger. Psalm 78 tells briefly how God saved the people of Israel from Egypt and provided for them in the desert and yet they continually rebelled against Him. In so doing they angered Him. Twice it says in verses 56 to 62 that "He was very angry." We do not like to think of God in this way, but the Bible clearly teaches there is such a thing as "the wrath of God." We can see what a terrible thing this is as we read Romans 1 verses 18 to 32. Rebellion against the authority of God damages and finally destroys all that is good and beautiful in His creation and this makes God very angry. On the other hand from our side there is alienation. Just as Absalom became separated from his father and went far away, so it is with us and God. It is said in Colossians 1:21 that we "were alienated from God and enemies in our minds because of evil behaviour." This left us "without God and without hope." [Ephesians 2:12] A desperate state indeed! We were lost and needed to be reconciled!

Jesus Reconciles us to God

The awful seriousness of rebellion makes reconciliation an all-important issue. This is especially shown in three places in the New Testament.

In the first passage, [Romans 5:6-11] we read that Christ died for sinners, for ungodly ones without power to do good, and for those who were God's enemies all needing to be reconciled and saved from His wrath. This was made possible "through the death of His Son."

In the second passage, [2 Corinthians 5:18-21] we see that reconciliation is something God has done. While we were sinners and rebels He took the initiative to reconcile us to Himself in Christ, by "not counting men's sins against them." He did something by which He could cancel the charge and restore us as though we had never rebelled. There was only one way this was possible. The charge against us had to be placed somewhere else and the penalty paid by someone else and this was done by Jesus, God's own Son, on the cross. "God made Him who had no sin to be sin for us that in Him we might become the righteousness of God." This was the only way we could be reconciled.

The third passage, [Colossians 1:19-22] goes still further. Here we read that God reconciled us "by Christ's physical body, through death," and "through His blood shed on the cross." We see three great steps in God's work of reconciliation. The first step was when the eternal Christ took a physical body like ours in which there would be no rebellious spirit. In the second step He identified Himself with us during His earthly life in our needs, our sufferings and our joys. In the final step He gave His body to be crucified and His blood to be poured out in a sacrificial death by which He made a perfect offering to God and an infinite restitution for all our rebellion. He was able to say in the words of Psalm 69:4 [A.V.] "I restored that which I took not away," and in the words of Isaiah 50:5,6 "I have not been rebellious, I have not drawn back." In His death He removed the cause of our alienation from God by being "pierced for our rebellions and crushed for our iniquities." [Isaiah 53:5] In this way Jesus completed the work of reconciliation.

The result of this perfect work is that we can have peace with God and access to Him. We can be free from guilt and fear so as to live in harmony with our heavenly Father, because we are "presented holy in God's sight without blemish and free from accusation." What a tremendous difference is made by such reconciliation. We do not have to work to achieve it. In the Cross the reconciling work has been accomplished and as we come to God in repentance and faith, we receive and enjoy this restored relationship able and ready to share the good news with others. [Romans 5:1S and Colossians 1: 21-23]

Jesus Reconciles us to One Another

There is however another aspect. The rift between God and Adam in the garden of Eden was soon followed by the murder of Abel by his brother Cain. So began a train of violence which eventually spread throughout the world. [Genesis 4:8 and 6:11] We not only need to be reconciled to God, but also to one another since it is in the area of relationships that most of our sinning occurs.

The problem is dealt with in Ephesians chapter 2 verses 11 to 22. When this was written, the world was hopelessly divided into national, cultural and religious camps - Romans against Greeks, Greeks against Barbarians and, worst of all, Jews against Gentiles. Everywhere there were walls of division. In verse 14 we read of "the barrier, the dividing wall of hostility." This refers to a wall in the court of the Jewish temple beyond which no Gentile dared pass for fear of death. It represented the enmity, contempt, hatred and hostility that existed between Jews and Gentiles. Is not the world still the same? Everywhere we find "walls" between people; in homes, families, communities and between nations.

Hostility - The Result of Sin

The root cause is always sin of some kind such as jealousy or resentment leading to hatred and revenge - all springing from selfishness, pride and the determination to have our own way. These are the results of the division between us and our Creator. How are they to be dealt with? only by the same cross that heals our relationship with God. In the death of Christ hostility has been destroyed because He has taken it upon Himself. Jesus bore all the hatred and hostility launched against Him by both Jews and Gentiles, as it says, "He endured such opposition from sinful men." [Hebrews 12:3] He took away the hostility by taking away the sin that caused our divisions in the first place. It says, 'We who were far away are brought near through the blood of Christ." This means we can be near to God and to one another as we find Jesus to be our peacemaker and are ourselves "reconciled in one body through the cross." [Eph: 2:11-18] In Christ all divisions are abolished so that there is now "no Greek nor Jew, Barbarian, Scythian, slave or free, but Christ is all and is in all." [Colossians 3:11]

In the Lord Jesus and His atoning sacrifice, God has dealt with everything that causes hostility. The Law of Moses need not divide us because Jesus has fulfilled it by His perfect obedience and also suffered the penalty for our breaking of that Law. Sin need not divide us, for it has been put away through the shedding of His blood. As for our sinful nature, it has been judged in Christ's crucified body so that we can be given a new nature in which we are united in the fellowship of the Holy Spirit. What a tremendous work of reconciliation God has accomplished through the Cross.

Why Still Divided?

Why then are we still divided when God has done everything to reconcile us? Is it not because we fail to recognise or take account of our hostile reactions? Consequently we do not repent or forgive and so do not avail ourselves of what is possible through the cross. Where we do repent however, even in a small matter, there breaks in at that point something of the great work of reconciliation just as sunshine pours through where there is even a tiny chink in the clouds.

When our children were small they would never go to bed without being kissed "goodnight." If they had been naughty they would come and say sorry to me. But sometimes if they had quarrelled with each other, they would still try to sit on my lap. Then I would say, "I will forgive you, but you must first forgive one another." When they did, there would be reconciliation sealed by hugs and kisses all round. In this way love and unity were maintained in the family.

The result of God's reconciling work is "to create one new man out of the two." This means where there have been two at enmity they are made one in unity. This is God's new creation, the church in which the Holy Spirit baptises us into one body where we all have access to our one Father in the fellowship of the one family. [Ephesians 2:15, 18]

In Old Testament times there was a special way of describing people who were alienated. It was said that their faces were "turned away" or were "not towards" one another as before. The message was clear: "Look out, there is trouble ahead!"

In the holiest room of the Tabernacle was the "mercy seat" where God said He would meet with His people and commune with them through their High Priest. over it were two golden angelic figures with outspread wings. They were bowed in worship above the blood of the sin offering sprinkled beneath them. The significant thing, however, was that their faces looked towards one another over the mercy seat while between them shone the "shekineh," the light of God's presence. They were always looking at each other over the atoning blood and through the holy light of God's glory. What a picture of fellowship! This is how God wants us to live with Him and with one another. [Exodus 25: 20]

My face has not always been "towards" others as it should have been. Even in my own family, I have often needed to bow in repentance and be reconciled. I still do. One of the boys who used to come to be kissed goodnight, began at one stage in his teenage years to be rude and rebellious. I slowly grew more and more irritated with him which did not improve our relationship. We began to be alienated. Then one day he came into the house and was cheeky to his mother in front of me. At this my anger boiled over and grabbing a cricket stump from some nearby sports gear, I lashed out at him in a rage and chased him up the stairs. He ran to his bedroom and slammed the door. Doreen gently rebuked me for my action and I retired to my study feeling badly upset. Getting on my knees I asked the Lord's forgiveness then went and told Doreen I had repented. She asked if I had peace. I said, "No" to which she replied, "I don't think you will until you go and repent to Christopher." I answered, "Certainly not, he deserves what he got." She replied "I thought you said you had repented. It doesn't sound much like it." So it was back to the study to pray a bit more until at last I realised I must go and be reconciled to my son. I went painfully up to his room and knocked at his door. No answer! I went in. He would not look at me. His face was hard and angry. Then the Lord helped me to say I was sorry for hitting him and I asked his forgiveness. He looked at me in utter surprise then burst into tears and took all the blame. We knelt down together, a pair of sinners, asked the Lord's forgiveness, forgave one another and came downstairs reconciled. From that moment our relationship was changed and what is more Chris began to lead the way in taking blame when anything went wrong in the home. All too often we Christians are afraid to trust the power of the blood of Jesus to cleanse from all sin, including that which arises in our relationships. Too often we are not willing to repent to one another. But the fact is there is power in the work of Calvary to reconcile not only sinners to God, but sinners to each other, so that we can live with faces turned to one another reflecting the light of God's glory.

At the Cross God turned His face away from His beloved Son that He might turn His face towards us, the sinners.

EIGHT | **God on our Side**

The army commander was being threatened. While his soldiers were preparing to storm an enemy fortress, he took a walk to view the situation when he was suddenly confronted by a man holding a drawn sword in his hand. Not certain who it was, he asked him, "Are you for us or for our enemies?" The man replied, "Neither, but as the commander of the army of the Lord I have now come." General Joshua, realising this was the angel of the Lord, at once accepted his leadership and there and then the future outcome of the battle of Jericho was settled. [Joshua 5: 13-15] The one whom Joshua feared was against him, he now discovered was for him.

Is God For Us or Against Us?

Sometimes we feel that God is against us. Often it seems so in the world of nature where although much is pleasant and beautiful, a great deal is harsh and hostile. Primitive peoples who live close to nature, and often feel at its mercy, are in constant fear of their gods and try in every way to placate them. We do not find much comfort in history either, for though there are bright ages and glorious achievements, they have been overshadowed by frightful horrors of every kind. So whether we look at nature or history, neither seems able to tell us whether God is for us or against us.

What about the Bible? Here we also find sunshine and shadow. The idyllic days of Eden gave place to the disastrous Flood. The good promises made to the patriarchs of Israel ended in long years of slavery and misery in Egypt. Was God for His people or not? The greatest revelation of Him was given in Exodus 34 where we read of God being "compassionate and gracious, abounding in kindness and faithfulness." Such all-embracing love seemed wonderful. Yet it was given against a background of thunder, lightning and burning fire that struck terror into those who were there.

God then gave Israel His Law in which He demanded righteousness and love. But since they were all sinners unable to fulfil His commandments they inevitably became burdened with guilt, and threatened with judgement. If they could only keep the Law they would be blessed, but if they broke it even at one point they were cursed. The effect was to make them feel that God was against them. In our society, if we obey the laws of the land, we are quite happy with the police. We know they are around to help and protect us. It is very different if we break a law, even one.

Police and Parents

I was once driving with the family through a town which I didn't know, looking for the address of a friend. As a result I lost my way. Then suddenly Doreen said, "There's a policeman, let's ask him." We drove down the road towards him and I asked with a smile, "Excuse me, officer, can you please tell me how to find So and So street?" Without returning my smile he calmly took a notebook out of his pocket saying, "You are driving the wrong way down a one way street! Name and address please." No mercy! He booked me straight away for an offence and I had to pay a fine. The one I thought was for me turned out to be against me. However he did then show me the way to my friend's house!

As a boy, I was brought up in a secure but strict home where my parents did everything for my good. But if I did wrong they punished me and when this happened I felt sure they did not love me but were against me. Yet actually it was I who was against them! When I was sorry I found they had been for me all along and were only acting for my good. I had two little sisters who were also naughty at times for which they would be punished and made to stay in their bedroom. After a while their howling would change to mournful singing. If mother had punished them, they would keep chanting, "My nice Daddy. My nice Daddy." If father had punished them, the duet would be, "My nice Mummy. My nice Mummy."

I used to find it very amusing. But you see the point - the one who did the punishing was not nice but was against them. The other parent was for them. But actually both were for them. Adam and Eve when they disobeyed God in the garden of Eden ran to hide from Him, quite convinced He was their enemy. We are the same. In our sinfulness we are sure God has something against us. And indeed He has if we do not repent.

What About Our Circumstances?

We may also think that God is against us when our circumstances are difficult. This is how Job felt when everything went wrong in his life. Disaster struck him on all sides and, pious man though he was, he railed against God saying, "He has made me His target and His archers surround me. Without pity He pierces me and rushes at me like a warrior." [Job 16:12-14] As for his friends, they believed that God, being good, was always on the side of good people and against bad ones and this showed up in their circumstances. They therefore concluded that Job must be very wicked and that God was against him.

Have you ever felt like this? Your world seems to have fallen apart and you cry out like Jacob long ago, "Everything is against me!" So God must be as well! [Gen. 42:36] At other times when overcome with guilt and failure you feel you are a prisoner in the dock with God sitting over against you like a judge on a bench. The case is sure to go against you. Your situation is hopeless and you are in despair. But then comes a surprising word from heaven, "If God be for us who can be against us?" [Romans 8:31] We ask, "Is God really for us? How is this possible?"

How Can God Be For Us?

God can be for us because He has sent Jesus. In Him He has crossed over from His judge's bench to stand with us in the dock without in any way compromising His justice. Everything about Jesus tells us that God who could rightly be against us has come to be for us. We see this in the birth of Jesus when He came from heaven to be one with us, in His baptism as He stood in the Jordan among the penitents and in His acceptance of sinners as He ate with them. We see it in His refusal to condemn a poor guilty woman whom the religious leaders would stone to death. And in His mercy towards outcasts and untouchables such as lepers and Samaritans. Then there are His parables such as the lost sheep, the prodigal son, the Pharisee and the Publican, and others. We also have His statements that He came "to seek and save the lost," came "not to be served but to serve and give His life a ransom for many." [Luke 15; 5:32. Mark 10:45]

In all these ways and words Jesus shows us that God is for us and not against us.

God For Us in the Cross

However, there is a paradox in the teaching of Jesus on this issue. He says on the one hand that He has come into the world "for judgement," yet on the other, that He "judges no one." [John 9:39 and 8:15] Can these be reconciled? Yes, because measured against His life and words we all stand judged. We are, as it were, "in the dock." Yet His purpose and desire is not to condemn us, for it says, "God did not send His Son into the world to condemn the world, but to save the world through Him." [John 3:17]

But how, you ask, can He the Holy One, who ought to be against us sinners, now be for us? Here is something neither nature, history nor human reason can demonstrate. Only the cross of Calvary can do this. There we see, as Paul says, that "God did not spare His only Son, but gave Him up for us all." [Romans 8:32] Much as the Father loved His Son He did not save Him from the cross, nor would Jesus save Himself as He could well have done. He had come there in order to take our place "in the dock," to bear our judgement at infinite cost so as to secure our acquittal.

> *He laid aside His reputation,*
> *When He came and stood by me;*
> *Willing to take the lowest station,*
> *When He came and stood by me.*

Yes, Jesus did come and stand by us - in His birth, His baptism, His life of love and above all His sacrifice on the cross where a criminal crucified beside Him found this to be true. This dying thief knew that all were against him, Roman authorities, religious leaders, the crowds who stood to watch him die. But he found, by his side, one whom he recognised to be the Lord of God's heavenly kingdom, yet to whom he could turn in repentance and with whom he found acceptance and welcome into Paradise. Jesus had come from heaven to hang on a cross beside him. In the same way He comes to stand with us and be for us in our sinfulness and deepest need.

How Do We Respond?

Paul asks the question, "what then shall we say in response to this?" [Romans 8:31] What can we say? What must we say? We cannot remain in stony silence. I know I need to say, "Lord I am sorry for my sins. I repent of all that caused Your suffering." How can I do otherwise in the light of the Cross? How can I harden my heart when His was broken for me? How can I cling to my own "righteousness" when He so willingly gave up His own? Charles Wesley put it like this in one of his hymns:

> *Give me the eye of faith to see*
> *The man transfixed on Calvary;*
> *To know Thee as Thou art,*
> *The one eternal God and true,*
> *And let that sight affect, subdue,*
> *And break my stubborn heart.*

Surely, if Jesus was willing to take His place by me on the cross, then I can only take my place before Him in repentance.

Paul writes, "What then shall we say in response to this? If God be for us, who can be against us?" Our answer must surely be that we repent of our sins. But we can also say that we find hope. The cross is the "door of hope" for sinners because Christ has died and risen again so that in God's courtroom we can be pronounced "not guilty." Again Paul says in verse 33 "Who shall bring any charge against those whom God has chosen? It is God who justifies." There is also hope because Christ intercedes for us in heaven so that there is always forgiveness for those who repent. Hope, because the Holy Spirit has been sent to give us new life and help us in our weaknesses. Hope, since "in all things God works for the good of those who love Him." [Romans 8:28] Hope, because "in all things we are more than conquerors through Him who loved us" and because "nothing in all creation will be able to separate us from the love of God in Christ Jesus our Lord." [Romans 8:35-39] What glorious hope, rising up from the cross! How can we ever doubt or despair when in all these things God is for us?

Is God Never Against Us?

Surely this is too good to be true? Is God never against us? He may be. He was certainly on the side of His people Israel when He saved them from Egypt and led them through the desert. Yet there came a time when "He turned and became their enemy and He Himself fought against them." [Isaiah 63:10] Here is a warning for us! God is totally and irrevocably against sin of every kind. Those who forsake their sins by turning to Him in repentance will find He is for them. Those who refuse to do so and remain wedded to their sins, will find in the last day that the One who came to be for them on His Cross will be against them on His Throne. That will be a fearful discovery.

Today, however, we can approach a different throne - "the throne of grace, so that we may receive mercy and find grace to help us in our time of need." [Hebrews 4:16]

Because of the cross there is pardon for every sin and power for all our weakness. One of my daughters, when she was little, took a liking to some of my special books which had very pretty dust covers. She would creep into my study when I was out, pull them from their shelves and strew the covers all over the floor. She was told again and again to leave them alone, but it made no difference. Finally came a warning of punishment. One day she came in again and had just taken out the first book when she heard a sound and turning round saw me watching her from my desk across the room. She looked about frantically and made for the door holding the book in her hands, then dropping it, she rushed over to me and with tears buried her head in my lap. I gathered her up in my arms and gave her a great big hug. She had been sure I would be against her. Instead she found I was all for her. She had given up the book and turned to me. She never touched those books again.

I have always remembered this incident and have often prayed "Lord help me let go forbidden things and never run to hide from You, but run to hide in You." You can pray that prayer as well.

Because Jesus died for your sins you need never fly from God in fear, but always run in faith to Him whose love will never fail.

NINE | Unfailing Love

The prophet Hosea was to be married. The circumstances were unusual because God had not only told him who to marry, but what kind of girl she would be. She would have the heart of a prostitute and be unfaithful to him. Knowing this, yet in obedience to God he married a girl called Gomer. They set up home and had three children. Everything seemed promising at first until Hosea found that God's word had come true. Gomer was going after other men and finally she left him for her rich lovers to live a life of selfish indulgence. This however did not last and she ended up destitute and for sale in a slave market. Yet in spite of everything, Hosea still loved her.

I do not know any situation which illustrates both the pain and the power of God's love like this story. It was recorded to show the kind of love God had for the people of Israel who, though called to live in a pure and perfect relationship with Him, like a "marriage bond," proved faithless by their worship of other gods. As a result they deteriorated so much that He allowed them to become captives in Babylon. Yet He loved them through it all and eventually restored them. Gomer's story was the story of Israel. But is it not also yours and mine? It is the story of God's undying love for sinners.

Judgment and Grace

The two prophets Amos and Hosea lived about the same time, but their messages were rather different. Amos had several visions of judgment in one of which God was seen with a plumbline in His hand testing the straightness of a wall. He was measuring the people of Israel by the standard of His Law only to find their life crooked beyond repair. Things had gone so far that judgment was inevitable. This was repeated in another vision of a basket of ripe fruit, showing that the time was ripe for judgment. You can read about these in Amos 7:7-9 & 8:1-2. Into this scene came Hosea looking for a way through the seemingly hopeless situation. Was there not a power which, while judging sin, could also displace and finally defeat it? He found the answer in the Grace of God. In a Love which, while it did not annul the Law, could somehow transcend it. The name "Hosea" is significant. It comes from the Hebrew word for "save" as do the names Joshua, Hoshea and Jesus. We can say that Hosea was a picture of God as the One who saves His people. This appears in several places in the book such as chapter 13 verse 14, where God says, "I will ransom them from the power of the grave; I will redeem them from death."

Hosea did not just preach his message, he lived it in the circumstances of his marriage and home life. He was a personal "sign" of God's love for the people in spite of their unfaithfulness towards him. This is not to say that Hosea had no message of judgment. He certainly had. He began by showing what a desperate thing sin is. How it is spiritual adultery that wounds the heart of God. Of the many figures for sin in the Bible, such as missing the mark, twisting what is straight and rebelling against authority, the most poignant of them all is that of wounding divine love by forsaking the divine Lover. The prophets Jeremiah and Ezekiel also describe this in vivid terms. The terrible thing about sin is the hurt we inflict on others, but most of all on God Himself. This is what is shown by the story of Hosea and Gomer and we see this ultimately in the cross of Christ.

Such sin inevitably brings judgment. We cannot hurt God without hurting ourselves and Hosea portrays this in dark colours. He says that sin produces rottenness and destruction. It results in abandonment to the selfish ways we choose and the evil things we do until we become like them. This, we can see today, has horrible effects in people's lives, as God says, "They consecrated themselves to that shameful idol and became as vile as the thing they loved." [Hosea 9: 10, 11, 16.] In the end God may have to leave us to our evil choices which lead only to despair and outer darkness. Yet this is far from Hosea's final word. His story is not of anger that forsakes, but of love that follows, always with the hope of recovery. The message of the book is about a God who will not let His chosen people go.

Marriage - Natural and Spiritual

God has a unique purpose for those He loves which is embodied in the covenant of marriage. In the closing scene of Hosea's domestic drama he buys back his faithless wife from her slavery and then says to her, "You shall stay with me and I will also be for you." [Hos: 3:3] I picture them going home hand in hand to find comfort and fulfilment in a renewed relationship. Surely this is what true marriage is all about. In the beginning God said, "It is not good for man to be alone. I will make a helper suitable for him. Then the Lord made a woman and brought her to the man." [Genesis 2: 18 & 22] The love that gave Eve to Adam is the same love that gives us to one another in our marriages, not only to be joined together, but to be kept together for the high purpose God has for us. We can understand this better when we see human marriage as a pattern of the covenant between God and Israel in the Old Testament and Christ and His church in the New. God spoke of Himself as the "husband" of His redeemed people in a union that was to bring blessing to the whole world. [Isaiah 54:5 and Jeremiah 3:14 and 31: 32.] In the New Testament, Christ is called the head of the church which is His bride. We are told that "Christ loved the church and gave Himself up for her, to make her holy, and present her to Himself a radiant church without stain or wrinkle or any other blemish, but holy and blameless." [Ephesians 5; 25-29] These wonderful words are fulfilled in the book of Revelation chapter 21 where "the bride the wife of the lamb" is seen "coming down out of heaven from God, beautifully dressed for her husband," and shining with the glory of God "like a very precious jewel, and like jasper clear as crystal." This dazzling picture describes the perfection for which the Lord has destined His church in the coming age, and towards which He is working even now in our daily lives. Love always seeks the perfection of the beloved. Marriage means mutual commitment, mutual fulfilment and mutual perfection!

Let us believe what the Scripture says - that we who belong to Jesus are loved and saved to be His eternal bride, to realise the great and gracious purposes God has planned for us and for mankind.

The Purity of God's Love

There is purity in God's love which is shown in Hosea's love for one who was so unworthy, one who would dishonour his name, shatter his marriage and break his heart. She would run after other men, sell herself to them for food and jewelry and end up as a harlot-slave in the public market. Yet Hosea would love her still, his only desire to do her good by restoring the original purpose of their marriage. Such is the love of God for us, untarnished by our violations of it and undeterred by the wounds we inflict on it. Charles Wesley put it this way:

> *I have long withstood His grace, Long provoked Him to His face,*
> *Would not hearken to His calls, Grieved Him by a thousand falls.*
> *Whence to me this waste of love? Ask my Advocate above!*
> *See the cause in Jesus' face, Now before the throne of grace. "*
> *There for me the Saviour stands;*
> *Shows His wounds and spreads His hands.*
> *God is love; I know, I feel; Jesus weeps and loves me still.*

Our human love is always tarnished by selfishness, but God's love is radiant with purity because He is perfect love.

The Pain of Wounded Love

Love inevitably suffers because of our sin. You can see this in Hosea chapter 2 [A.V.] where the heart-broken husband cries out to his children, "Plead with your mother, plead with her." The N.I.V. translates it, "Rebuke your mother." The very pleading of Hosea carries with it a warning and rebuke to the one he loves so much. We see him reeling under the blows, crushed by the sorrow of his shattered hopes. There is no pain so deep as that of wounded love, no desolation so dark as that of the forsaken lover. In all this, Hosea felt something of the love of God who says of His people,"How well I remember those first delightful days when I led you through the wilderness. How refreshing was your love! How satisfying! But then you deserted me...to give yourselves to other gods and soon you were as foul as they." [Ch.9:10 Living Bible.] In Jeremiah 2:1-5 God says "I remember the devotion of your youth, how as a bride you loved me and followed me through the desert. What fault did your fathers find in me, that they strayed so far from me? They followed worthless idols and became worthless themselves." Do you not feel the pathos in these words and sense the suffering of the divine Lover? Do you not see yourself in the picture as I can see myself at times, leaving the love I first had for the Lord, straying from Him, growing hard and cold towards Him and in this way violating His covenant with me?

The Tension Between Love and Judgment

The suffering love of God comes to its climax in Hosea 11:8. I shall refer to this again in the next chapter. ["The Cross in the Heart of God,"] See how the prophet's story depicts God's relationship with us. How condemnation of sin is in tension with love that would forgive the sinner. The dilemma in the heart of Hosea is there in God Himself. We find throughout the book how the black clouds of judgment are pierced through with the bright rays of compassion. Eventually God cries out as though in a turmoil, "oh, how can I give you up my Ephraim? How can I let you go? How can I forsake you? My heart cries out within me. How I long to help you. No, I will not punish you as much as my fierce anger tells me to. I am the Holy One living among you, and I did not come to destroy." [Living Bible; Hos. 11:8] God's love which began as ecstasy has now become agony. This is what the cross of Calvary shows us. It is the focal point in time where God's justice and love resolved their age-long tension in the sacrifice of Christ. There, in order to spare us our just condemnation, the Father gave up His only Son to suffer in our place. Many rays of truth in the Bible focus on this mystery. In the New Testament the most penetrating is in 2 Corinthians 5:21 where it says, "God made Him [Christ] who had no sin, to be sin for us, so that in Him we might become the righteousness of God." There, in one phrase, is summed up what God did for us in Christ on the cross However much I ponder this I can never fully grasp its mystery. Katherine Kelly, the hymn writer, says:

> *O make me understand it;*
> *Help me to take it in,*
> *What it meant to Thee, the Holy one,*
> *To bear away my sin."*

As I see Jesus dying there for me I can only believe what the Scripture has revealed, that in this mighty Act, God in both His holiness and His love confronted evil "head-on" in order to come to grips with the sin of the world. This meant infinite suffering on the part of both the Father and the Son. Yet it was fruitful suffering because of the victory it achieved. Our sin was atoned for, by the precious blood that flowed from Calvary. We can never think lightly about the cross when we see how God suffered because His love would not abandon us to condemnation, yet His holiness had to give His beloved Son, Jesus, to be judged in our place. It was the only way God could answer His own cry, "oh, how can I give you up, my Ephraim?"

The "Again" of God's Love

Another feature of God's love as we see it in Hosea is its persistence, centred in two short words, "Go... again." In chapter 3 verse 1 God tells the prophet "Go show your love to your wife again although she is an adulteress. Love her as the Lord loves the Israelites though they turn to other gods." Hosea loved her when she was virgin pure. Now he is to show his love to her again when she is defiled and degraded. This is the message of chapter 2 where God is shown following Israel, His erring wife, through her profligate paths, blocking her way with thorns, stripping her of all her ill-gotten gains to bring her at last to a lonely desert place, not to destroy her, but to speak tenderly to her so as to renew their marriage and restore what she had lost. It is this persistence of God that led George Matheson to write the words of the hymn:

> *O love that will not let me go;*
> *I rest my weary soul in Thee;*
> *I give Thee back the life I owe,*
> *That in Thine ocean depths its flow*
> *May richer, fuller be.*

Another poet, Francis Thompson, who had been found by God after years of wandering from Him, wrote a poem called, "The Hound of Heaven" in which God is pictured relentlessly pursuing the fugitive soul until, stripped of everything, it is brought to bay, only to hear God the divine Lover say:

> *Whom wilt thou find to love ignoble thee*
> *Save Me, save only Me?*
> *All that I took from thee I did but take,*
> *Not for thy harms*
> *But just that thou might's seek it in My arms.*
> *All that thy child's mistake fancies as lost,*
> *I have stored for thee at home:*
> *Rise, clasp My hand and come.*

Hope in the Valley

Such was the story of Hosea and Gomer. In obedience to God's word the prophet went again to show his love to his faithless wife. He found her up for sale in a slave market, degraded almost beyond recognition and when the bidding started he was first in the queue to buy her. She went under the hammer for half the price of a slave plus a day's ration of food, so low had she sunk. And what then? No longer to be a slave or a harlot, but to come home redeemed and changed that she might live with her husband once more in renewed love. A door of hope had been opened in her "Valley of Trouble." [Hos. 2:15]

There has never been a valley of trouble like that which the Lord Jesus entered when in Gethsemane He prayed, "If it is possible, let this cup pass from me." [Matt. 26: 39 A.V.] It was not possible, for there was no other way for us to be saved. But love went through that dark valley making it a door of hope for all to find. Hosea paid a paltry price for his fallen bride. But He went and paid it. Jesus paid an enormous price - His own life-blood. A great price was given because the giver was so great. He gave Himself to be the ransom. Hosea's pilgrimage of love amazes us, but it was nothing to the journey Jesus took from the heights of His heavenly glory to the depths of the cross because of His love and determination to save and restore us.

Love That Prevails

But the story does not end there. Hosea's love prevailed. So it is with the love of God. Sin may rule, but grace overrules and the message of Hosea is of "mighty grace o'er sin abounding," of love that does what law can never do. And what does love do? For one thing it brings people to repentance. In chapter 6 we find the sinful people saying, "Come let us return to the Lord. He will heal us, bind up our wounds, restore us." Repentance seems superficial here, but it is at least a beginning. In chapter 14 however, it becomes a cry from the heart, "O Lord take away our sins; be gracious to us and receive us and we will offer you the sacrifice of praise. Never again will we call the idols we have made 'our gods' for in you alone, O Lord, the fatherless find mercy." [Living Bible.] Here is real repentance.

Is this what happened to Hosea's prodigal wife? Did she repent when she saw her own husband coming into the market place to rescue her from her fearful plight? Was it the discovery that he loved her at her very worst? Surely it was his grace that broke and changed her.

It is the same for me. I remember at one time becoming hard in heart because of pride. As a result I began to be harsh towards my wife over trivial matters while justifying myself for my behaviour. One day I spoke very unkindly to her and then went into my study to prepare for a meeting. I found myself reading Philippians chapter 2 which I almost knew by heart. But on this occasion I saw Jesus as never before, coming from His glory to go to the cross. I read again and again the words, "He humbled Himself to death even death on a cross," and as I did so I was convicted of my sinful pride and my hard heart was melted. Then what could I do but repent and ask Doreen to forgive me. Nothing brings repentance like the sight of Jesus going to Calvary to pay the price for our sin.

Changed By Love

True repentance will always affect our life and behaviour. We return to the Lord in order to remain in Him. Gomer, when she had been ransomed, went home to live with Hosea and he with her. In chapter 14:7 we see the penitent people coming to rest under the shadow of their God so as to flourish and bloom like a fruitful garden. In the end love not only conquers, but changes us. The cross and the resurrection are the true fulfilment of the Hosea story. Only at Calvary can we see this pure and persistent love of God for sinners which will always draw us back to our Lord in repentance and thanksgiving.

Jesus on the cross pours out love - marvellous love shown to cruel men, implacable enemies and faithless friends. Love to a dying thief. A broken hearted mother. Love to sinners like you and me. But it is victorious love, for as Hosea went down to the slave-market, the ransom price in his hand, to come up again with his wife by his side, so Jesus went down into death and rose again, in His hand the marriage contract for the church He came to purchase with His own blood. We are the objects of unfailing love. Love that will not let us go. How can we do other than respond with all our hearts to such a divine Lover.

> *Have you heard Him, seen Him, known Him?*
> *Is not yours a captured heart?*
> *Chief among ten thousand own Him,*
> *Joyful choose the better part.*
>
> *What has stripped the seeming beauty*
> *From the idols of the earth?*
> *Not the sense of right or duty,*
> *But the sight of peerless worth.*

Not the crushing of those idols,
With its bitter void and smart;
But the beaming of His beauty,
The unveiling of His heart.

'Tis that look that melted Peter,
'Tis that face that Stephen saw;
'Tis that heart that wept with Mary,
Can alone from idols draw.

Draw and win and fill completely,
Till the cup o'erflow the brim.
What have we to do with idols
Who have companied with Him?

TEN | The Cross in the Heart of God

We all know that the symbol of our Christian faith is the Cross of Christ, but do we understand what it means? Many think only of material objects made of wood or metal in the form of a cross which many believe has mystical powers when touched or used as a sign. There is no Biblical basis for this and it easily leads to superstition.

For some the historical event of the crucifixion was a tragedy. A great and good man cruelly put to death through prejudice, envy and fear. Many regard it as the great example of passive resistance, while others think in terms of its moral influence, teaching us how to suffer and die for our convictions. Above all it is considered a beautiful ideal of self-sacrificing love. These views all have an element of truth in them yet they suffer from a basic defect in that they only emphasise what is either historical or human. The "cross-event" is all in the hands of man, it is limited to a point in time and something to be admired or used as an example.

The Bible however shows it to be far more than this: that Christ crucified is the power and the wisdom of God. There is saving power in the cross which is completely missed in the inadequate views mentioned above. We must therefore look beyond these to see what a profound mystery is the death of Christ. We must go beyond man to God and out of time into eternity. We need to see that the cross was first in the heart of God, before it was ever in the minds of prophets or the experience of men. What do we mean by it being in God's "heart"?

The Cross in God's Purpose

The Cross of Christ was not an accident nor did it come about merely by the designs of men. On the contrary, it was in the intention of God, foretold and even described in prophecies throughout the old Testament such as Genesis 3:15, Psalms 22 and 69, Isaiah 53, Zechariah 13, Daniel 9 and in many other places. Jesus Himself said, "Did not Christ have to suffer these things and enter into His glory? And beginning with Moses and all the prophets He explained to them what was said in all the Scriptures concerning Himself." [Luke 24: 26, 27] Again and again the Lord Jesus foretold His own death. He said, "The Son of man must be lifted up" and again, "Destroy this temple and in three days I will raise it up." { John 3:14 and 2:19] In Matthew's gospel alone there are no fewer than twelve occasions when Jesus prophesied that He would die. The cross was certainly foretold. But why? The answer is that it was ordained by God. As Jesus said, "The Son of man goes [i.e. to the cross] as it has been determined." [Luke 22:22] The apostles also were clear about this. In Acts 2:23 Peter, when preaching at Pentecost, says of Jesus, "This man was handed over to you by God's set purpose and foreknowledge and you put Him to death nailing Him to the Cross." In Acts 4:28 when praying to God about those who had crucified the Lord, the disciples said, "They did what Your {God's} power and will had decided beforehand should happen." Again in Acts 17:3 Paul reasoned with the Jews from the Scriptures "explaining and proving that Christ had to suffer and rise from the dead." This is repeated in Galatians 1:4 in words about Christ, "He gave Himself [on the cross] for our sins, according to the will of our God and Father." All of which is enough to show us that the cross was in the heart and purpose of God before ever time began. However there is still something else.

God Involved in the Cross

The Cross was an event in which God was involved. This does not mean that the Father died at Calvary as some second century heretical church leaders taught.

However, Jesus said on many occasions, "The Father is with me." Wherever He was, there was God. In His incarnation He was called "Emmanuel" meaning "God with us." In John's gospel we are told that Christ the Word was with the Father in eternity and the Father was with Him here on earth. [John 1:1 & 2, 2:14 and 3:2] God was totally involved with His Son all through His life and ministry. But, you may ask, how was He with Him in the cross?

God - Light and Love

A church in the North of England, where I was minister for eight years, had galleries on which two texts were inscribed. On one side were the words, "God is Light," and on the other "God is Love." They happened to be two of the first verses I learned as a small boy in Sunday School and they had now come to face me each Sunday as I preached!

"God is Light" means that He is holy and pure. There is no darkness of evil in His person or presence. That is why in the Old Testament He showed Himself in the form of fire and why those who encountered Him were overwhelmed with awe and fear. One prophet, Habakkuk, said, "Your eyes are too pure to look on evil; you cannot tolerate wrong." [Hab. 1:13] Since God cannot accept or condone what morally offends His perfect nature, we can understand that He must react in judgment against everything sinful and selfish. This truth comes in many places in the Bible especially in such words as "God did not spare." We read that He did not spare angels who sinned, nor the corrupt and violent world in Noah's day. He did not spare the Egyptians who refused to let Israel go, nor even His chosen people, the

Jews, when they gave themselves to idol worship.

We are also warned to take care lest He does not spare us either. [See 2 Peter 2:4, Psalm 78:50, Romans 11:21.] As flames consume stubble, so the fire of God's holiness burns in judgment against evil and cannot spare those who refuse to be separated from their sin. This is what it means that "God is Light." The holiness of God can only have one basic reaction to sin, which is to reveal it and judge it.

God's Love for His Son

The other text on the gallery was "God is Love." Perfect love! Powerful and creative love! He loves all He has made and has to act against everything that harms His creation. Yet His love is never out of keeping with His holiness.

Could there be anyone God loves beyond those He created? Yes there is! The apostle John shows us who it is, in the profound words, "In the beginning was the Word [Christ] and the Word was with God and the Word was God. Through Him all things were made." [John 1: 1-3] Later he says in verse 16, "The only begotten Son who is at the Father's side has made Him known." Jesus could not have been closer to God than this. Also in the same Gospel, Jesus says "The Father loves the Son and has placed everything in His hands." [John 3. 35] Later He prayed to God, "You loved me before the creation of the world." [John 17:24.] Think of what this means. God loved His Son before anyone or anything was made and when Jesus came to earth God said, "You are my Son whom I love; with you I am well pleased." [Mark 1:11] Jesus is described as "The image of the invisible God," [Colossians 1:15] because in Him everything is consistent with God's nature and therefore draws out God's love in a unique manner and in full measure.

God's Love for Sinners

At the same time, the very Gospel that speaks so much of God's love for Christ also emphasises His love for men and women. We are created to be loved by God so that we might know and love Him in return. In John 3:16 we find the well-known words, "God so loved the world," words which lie at the heart of redemption. But we have violated His love to such an extent that He has been obliged to condemn us. And yet He loves us still.

God's Great Dilemma

Here then are two opposing factors. On the one hand is Holiness which demands judgment and banishment; on the other hand is Love that longs for reconciliation and fellowship. This is what I might call God's great dilemma. The question is, how can He resolve it? And how can we understand it?

We dare not speak lightly on so awesome a subject. But we find it illustrated in the story of Hosea and his wife as we saw in the previous chapter. ["Unfailing Love."]

The prophet's problem over his loved yet faithless wife was a picture of God's dilemma over His beloved people, Israel, who had forsaken Him for idols. In Hosea 11 verses 8 and 9, God cries out, "How shall I give you up, Ephraim? How can I hand you over, Israel?" [that is to destruction] This is what they deserve. But then follows the crisis of God's suffering, "My heart is changed within me: all my compassion is aroused. I will not carry out my fierce anger." Can you see the situation? Holiness demands that their sin be punished, but love longs to spare them. In one place God says, "My anger is kindled [made to burn] against them." [Hos. 8: 5] But now He says, "My compassions are kindled together. " [Hos. 11:8]

Here, "kindled" is a stronger word meaning "contracted," in spasm. Deeply affected! God is shown as suffering because of the tension between His justice and His love, so that He cries out, "How can I give you up. I will not! I will not!"

What a picture we have here of God's greater dilemma. He has infinite love for His Son, but He also loves the world of sinners. Jesus merits all the Father's favour. Sinners deserve all His anger. Here comes the crisis. One or other must be given up to judgment, yet both are loved. Whom shall God spare - the sinners or the Son? The answer is given us in Romans 8:32, "He did not spare His only Son, but gave Him up for us all." Listen to the Father's words when Jesus stands in His baptism of dedication in Jordan, "This is my beloved Son in whom I am well pleased." Then hear the cry of Jesus in His baptism of death on Calvary, "My God, My God, why have You forsaken me?" God had to forsake His beloved Son if He was to forgive sinners. on the Cross Christ's body was torn; but so was God's heart. Jesus was giving up His life. God was giving up His Son. Both were suffering. God was involved in the Cross.

> *O love of God; O sin of Man*
> *In this dread Act your strength is tried,*
> *And victory remains with Love.*
> *Jesus our Lord was crucified.*

God - Active in the Cross

There is yet a third factor. It is that in the cross, God was doing a stupendous work making it possible for the sins of the world to be taken away. He was dealing with sin by condemning it. I think the most profound truth in the Bible about the cross is given in 2 Corinthians 5:21 where it says that, "God made Him who had no sin to be sin for us so that in Him we might become the righteousness of God." We are told that Jesus took our sins on the cross, but this verse says that God the Father made Him to be sin. As Isaiah 53:6 puts it, "The Lord has laid on Him the iniquity of us all." In doing so, He was judging our sins and Jesus was willingly taking our judgment so that we might be justified or pronounced "not guilty." We shall see in a later chapter how the Scripture shows this to be possible.

It was a mighty act to create the world, but a mightier act to reconcile those who had defiled that world and become alienated from their Creator. We do not read of any suffering incurred in the act of creation. God only needed to speak and it was done. Light broke through and the Creator's heart was filled with joy. But the act of redemption involved the most intense suffering.

When Jesus died, the skies were black and the Father's face was hidden in grief. Yet out of this came something greater than a human race on a planet. God brought into being through the cross a new creation of men and women and the promise of a new heaven and a new earth. At Calvary God released the fullness of His love to sinners by giving up His beloved Son to die for our sins.

The cross which had always been in the heart of God has been fully shown to us in the life and death of Christ and as we acknowledge our dependence on His great work of salvation then surely the cross must be in our heart as the governing principle of all our behaviour.

ELEVEN | # The Cross in the Life of Jesus

You may know of a picture painted by Holman Hunt the Pre-Raphaelite artist showing the boy Jesus at work in the carpenter shop in Nazareth. Having put down His tools, He stands looking up to heaven stretching tired arms above His head. The sun is shining through the door and in doing so casts the boy's shadow on to a horizontal bar in the background so that it looks as though His hands have been nailed there. The picture is called "The Shadow of Death," reminding us that the cross was to affect His whole life.

"The Cross," as we have said, is much more than a wooden gibbet; more than a historical event on the "green hill far away." It signifies the great eternal sacrifice of Christ which was in the heart and purpose of God the Father to be accomplished in history by God the Son. We shall look in this chapter first at the cross as the purpose of Christ's coming into the world and second as the principle of His life in the world.

The Purpose of the Coming of Jesus

We have seen in a previous chapter that Christ existed with God even before the world was created. Although He was born of a mother, as we all are, He was different in that He came specially into the world from God. He Himself said this on many occasions and other scriptures bear it out. But why did He come? There are two specific statements concerning this.

The first is in Hebrews 10 verses 5-7 which says that when Christ came into the world He said, "Here I am - it is written about me in the scroll - I have come to do your will O God." The writing referred to is Psalm 40 which was a prophecy by king David about Christ who came primarily to do the will of God, a fact which Jesus Himself repeated in His lifetime.

But, we may ask, what was this "will of God ?" It was, as we have seen, to save sinners from their sins and this involved the atoning sacrifice of Jesus on the cross.

The second statement is found in Matthew 20:28 where Jesus specifically says that He had come "not to be served but to serve and to give His life a ransom for many." The term ransom means a price paid in order to free a captive and Jesus gave His unique life to liberate us from the bondage of sin. He came, as He said, "to seek and save what was lost." [Luke 19:10] He had come to teach us how to live, to reveal the Father to us in His person and life and to do God's works of mercy and judgment. But beyond all this He had come to die for our salvation. Again and again He spoke of His inevitable death - some twelve times in Matthew alone. See how He rebuked Peter who repudiated the idea of the cross. [Matthew 16: 21-23] Jesus was always looking towards what He called His "hour" - the supreme event of His atoning death on the cross. In John 12:27 He spoke of this and said, 'What shall I say? Father save me from this hour? No, it was for this very reason I came to this hour." It is quite clear then, that from all eternity the face of the Son of God was set towards Calvary because He had the same purpose as the Father - the salvation of sinners. Let us examine this carefully.

Storing or Sowing

I once had a glass phial in which were a number of small black objects. They were grains taken from a buried store of wheat, dating from the time of the Roman occupation. It was wheat alright, most of the grains still in perfect shape, but they had long since turned into charcoal. Some farmer had stored them for safety and in doing so had lost them. Had they been sown he would have reaped a harvest. As it was, they had never fulfilled their purpose. In John 12: 24 Jesus says in relation to Himself, "Unless a kernel of wheat falls to the ground and dies, it remains only a single seed. But if it dies, it produces many seeds." The farmer who only stores his corn will eventually lose it whether through mice or mildew or simply the passage of time. The man who sows his corn, willing to lose it in the dark damp earth, will find it multiplied in a succession of harvests. Jesus then gives us two options. We can "love" our life, so that we hold on to it selfishly. In that case we will lose its true value and meaning. On the other hand we can "hate" our life which means we give it up to Someone far greater than ourselves. Then we will keep it to eternal life. Jesus was willing to let go His life completely. This is what we mean by the principle of the Cross. Here are some areas of His life where this principle was worked out.

Giving Up His Own Interests

The first was in regard to His own interests. We all naturally look after our interests and consider it to be our right to do so. We think it is necessary for our well being and our survival. If anyone was entitled to His own interests, surely it was the Son of God. Yet His concern was always for the interests of others, and above all for the interests of God His Father. We read in Romans 15:2 and 3 that "each of us should please his neighbour for his good," and then it adds, "For even Christ did not please Himself." Whether in His temptations by the devil, the adulation of the crowds, the demands on His life, the sorrows and joys of every day, or finally the horror of the cross itself, His whole concern was always to do what pleased His heavenly Father and blessed His fellow men. The verdict given about Him as He hung on the cross was, "He saved others, Himself He could not save." Could not because He would not! Jesus was the man who lived and died wholly for others.

Giving Up His Own Will

By nature we all do what we want to do and are often angry when we are frustrated. We "turn every one to his own way," as it says in Isaiah 53, and this is our sin.

Jesus was the only one whose will was wholly given up to God's will. We all like our food. I do and I am sure the Lord Jesus did. But His real "food" He said, was "to do the will of Him who sent me and finish His work." [John 4: 34] That was more satisfying to Him than any earthly meal. We often go to great lengths to do what we want, but Jesus said, "I have come down from heaven not to do my will but to do the will of Him who sent me." [John 6:38] He knew what God's will involved. It was that sinners should be saved; that all whom the Father had given Him would come to Him and eventually a great harvest of souls reaped. In all this, Jesus delighted to do God's will even though it involved the cross. He said, "I lay down my life... no one takes it from me, but I lay it down on my own accord... This command I received from my Father." [John 10:17,18] We cannot comprehend the horror of what it meant for one who was the sinless Son of God to bear the sin of the world. Yet when He came to face the final moment, He said, "Father, not my will but Yours be done." [Luke 22:42] Right to the very end Jesus did God's will. Not His own.

Giving Up His Own Glory

Everyone likes to be praised. Children thrive on it and adults also need to be appreciated and affirmed. Some of us even go out of our way to court the praise of others, thinking we cannot function properly without it. We like to be well thought of, spoken of with approval and given honour. But how do we react when we meet with the opposite? When treated even with indifference? None of us can easily bear rejection. But that is what Jesus endured from the world. It says, "He came to that which was His own [world] but His own [people] did not receive Him." [John 1:11] The prophet Isaiah speaks of Him as "despised and rejected of men," and as one who "did not hide His face from mocking and spitting." In John 8:49 Jesus said to the religious leaders of His time, "You dishonour me." How was it, we may ask, that He who was worthy of all honour could accept such treatment? Because, as He said, He was not seeking glory for Himself, but only the honour of His Father. [See John 5:41 and 8: 49, 50] His one concern was to glorify God and in this He was in utter contrast to another who in his selfish pride said, "I will make myself like the Most High" and "raise my throne above the stars of God," only to be expelled from the divine presence and "brought down to the depths of the pit." We read the account of this in Ezekiel 28: 12-17 and Isaiah 12-17.

While these passages describe the arrogant rulers of Babylon and Tyre, they obviously refer to one far beyond them called Lucifer [The Lightbearer] "anointed as a guardian cherub." You will also find passages in the New Testament which tell of Satan "falling from heaven," being "hurled down" from God's presence and coming under condemnation through his conceit. Finally there was his demand that the very Son of God fall down and worship him. [See Luke 10:18, Revelation 12:10, 1 Timothy 3:6 and Matthew 4:9] Satan used his position to exalt himself. Jesus used His to humble Himself as vividly described in Philippians 2 verses 6 to 9. Contrast this with the passages in Isaiah and Ezekiel and see how the one who exalted himself was abased, while the One who humbled Himself was exalted. Satan was cast down to the lowest hell. Jesus was raised to the highest heaven.

This principle is stated three times in the gospels: "Everyone who exalts himself will be humbled and he who humbles himself will be exalted." [Matthew 23:12, Luke 14:11 and 18:14] Echoes of this truth resound through the Scriptures. Lucifer, the anointed angel, had his heart set on the Throne. He grasped after the highest honour. Jesus the eternal Son had His heart set on the Cross. He accepted the lowest dishonour with all its attendant suffering. "He endured the cross, despising the shame." [Hebrews 12:2] He "suffered outside the camp," which as we saw in chapter 1 was the place where criminals were stoned, lepers were left to suffer, garbage was dumped and bodies of animals were burned. [Heb. 13:11-13] It was no pleasant spot "outside a city wall where the dear Lord was crucified." It was a place of hatred and horror, of shame and stench. The lowest place!

This is where He chose to come in order to save sinners. The Cross!

Giving Up His Own Power

There was also the question of His own power. We love to have some kind of power, whether it is over people or circumstances. Power to cope or to control. And in a sense this is right. "You made him [man] ruler over all the works of your hands," says Psalm 8. In the beginning God said, "Let us make man, and let them rule over all the earth." [Genesis 2:26] We were made to be the head of creation which means power. What is wrong is that sin has corrupted this God-given gift of power so that instead of using it under God's authority and for His glory, we have perverted it to selfish ends. What was intended to be a blessing has been turned into a curse.

Jesus had supreme power. In three passages, [John 1, Colossians 1 and Hebrews 1] we are told how mighty He was as creator and sustainer of the universe. We would never have imagined this if the Scripture had not stated it. Something of that power showed itself on earth when Jesus created wine and bread, stilled storms, healed sicknesses, reversed decay and raised the dead. Satan, when tempting Him in the wilderness, encouraged Him to use His power for selfish ends. Jesus did not yield. Four times in John's gospel it says He disclaimed all use of power apart from God. He relied entirely on His

Father and did nothing by Himself. [John 5:19,30] In coming to earth He had taken on human weakness. In His earthly life He often experienced hunger, thirst, exhaustion and distress and as He moved to the end of life He faced increasing suffering and pain, until the climax came at Calvary where as we read, "He was crucified in weakness." [2 Corinthians 13:4] I never knew what real weakness was until I had open heart surgery. Then, while utterly helpless, too weak even to breathe without a ventilator, I thought, "This is how my Saviour must have felt as He hung on the cross." But I am only a weak man. He was the mighty Son of God, who for our sakes had become utterly helpless, drained of all strength. As Psalm 22 prophetically says of Him - "I am poured out like water, my strength is dried up like a potsherd and you lay me in the dust of death." How incredibly weak He became!

Yet that was not all. There was something more He gave up at Calvary.

Giving Up His Own Righteousness

What of His Righteousness? The word means "being right." We all love to be right, do we not? Indeed we will argue, fight, lose hours of sleep, blame everyone and everything to prove we are in the right. Look at Job in the Bible. As good a man as you could find, who, when he lost everything, accepted it all as God's will. One thing, however, he was not willing to give up and that was his own sense of being a righteous man. This he fought for in all the discussions with his friends, until at the end he had to face God. Then he saw himself as the sinner he was and repented "in dust and ashes." So it is for all of us. The hardest thing to let go is our claim to be in the right. We hate to admit we are wrong. Yet God says, "There is no one righteous, not even one. There is no difference for all have sinned and fall short of the glory of God." [Romans 3: 10, 22, 23.]

The fact is the only perfectly righteous person who has ever lived is Jesus. He is called in the Bible, "My righteous Servant, Jesus

Christ the Righteous One." Yet He who was wholly right in all He was and did, was willing to be regarded as wholly wrong on the cross. He who had become a man and yet had no sin "was made sin for us" and so became a sin offering, taking the penalty for our wrongdoing, even becoming "a curse for us" by hanging on a tree. [See 2 Cor. 5:21 and Gal. 3:13]

All this is shown in Philippians 2: 6-8, especially in the words, "He made Himself nothing" or as the hymn says, "Emptied Himself of all but love, and died for Adam's helpless race." In His death Jesus gave up everything by a final act of self surrender. The important thing is that His actions were always the result of His attitude. The Cross had been the governing principle of His existence in eternity as well as in time. Jesus was "The Lamb of God" long before He climbed the hill of Calvary.

Jesus - The Perfect One

What is the significance of all this? First, it means that the Lord Jesus is the perfect Saviour for us sinners because He is the perfect Sacrifice for our sins. He was "a Lamb without blemish or defect." [1 Peter 1:19] Had there been one vestige of selfishness in Him, He could never have saved us. In order to do so, He had to go to the Cross as the sinless sacrifice so as to bear our sins.

It means too that Jesus is the supreme Victor because He has overcome the power of evil. In Himself He is the complete opposite to all that Satan is. He was able to say, "The prince of this world has no hold on me." [John 14: 30] There was no ground within Him where the Devil could gain a foothold. Jesus could therefore be an acceptable offering to a holy God.

The principle of the Cross also means that Jesus is a perfect Example to us. Peter writes about this in his first epistle chapter 2 verse 21: "Christ suffered for you leaving you an example that you should follow in His steps." Paul says the same in Philippians 2:5: "Your attitude should be the same as that of Christ Jesus." He then describes this "attitude" in terms of the Cross.

How can we ever be like Jesus in this matter? He was unique! His work was perfect! It is surely impossible for us to follow Him Yet this is God's purpose - that "we should be conformed to the likeness of His Son." [Romans 8:29] It does not happen overnight. It is a lifelong process, a perpetual course of training in which we are told "Let us fix our eyes on Jesus... who endured the cross, scorning the shame. Consider Him... so that you will not grow weary." [Hebrews 12: 2 and 3]

The Cross in Our Lives

This is the special work of the Holy Spirit. His concern is to focus our eyes on Christ and then to engrave the Cross in our lives. It may be easy to wear the form of a cross around our necks, but quite another thing to know the experience of the cross in our hearts. Paul says in 2 Corinthians 4:10, "We always carry around in our body the death of Jesus so that the life of Jesus may also be revealed in our body." Mysterious words! Whatever do they mean? The early Christians suffered persecution and martyrdom, Paul more than any. He says again, "I bear on my body the marks of Jesus," probably referring to the scars of the many beatings and scourgings He had received. He suffered in His body, as did many others, but deeper than this was the imprint of the cross on His character and lifestyle. How little we know of this. We are not persecuted as Paul was. For the most part we live in safety and comfort and I, for one, who know virtually nothing of what it means to suffer for Christ, feel so unfit to write on such a theme. Yet, as we shall see in the following chapters, there are many ways in which we must know the principle of the cross in our daily life. It was the way our Lord went and in which He leads us all. Not in a negative way, but positive. One which means a daily death to self so that there may grow in us, and show through us, the life of the risen Christ. This is the will of God for us, gloriously possible by the saving power of the Cross and the presence and activity of the Holy Spirit within us.

TWELVE | # The Cross and Salvation

On my first preaching tour in the United States I was at a meeting in a Midwest farming town, speaking from Isaiah chapter 30, where Israel was threatened with invasion. I started by saying "The people of Israel were faced with a problem," at which a farmer in the congregation chimed in with, "That's nothing, Mister, we all got problems"! True enough! We've all got problems! The world is full of them. In marriages, families, homes, societies and among nations. Problems of every kind and in every place. We spend no end of time coping with and trying to solve them.

G.K. Chesterton was once asked, "What is wrong with this world?" He answered, "I am." In this honest answer he only echoed what the Bible makes clear that, from God's standpoint, the world's greatest problem is mankind's own sin. This is what Christ came to solve by dying on the cross.

Why is Sin the Problem?

Problems arise when things made to work smoothly and harmoniously together get out of kilter. Men and women were created to have a right relationship with God and with one another. This is the picture we see in Eden in Genesis chapter three. God made us for rightness, or as the Bible calls it, "righteousness." But, as we know, things went horribly wrong so that within a few generations the whole earth had become "corrupt in God's sight and full of violence." [Genesis

6:11] Nor is the situation any better when we come to the New Testament where it says, "There is no one righteous, not even one." [Romans 3:10] Then follows a vivid picture of human sinfulness which we have to admit is true of us today and from which inumerable problems arise in all areas of life.

Missing the Mark

You will have seen already from previous chapters how the Bible never treats sin lightly. But do we understand what sin is? There are about twenty different words in the original languages of the Scriptures describing sin in every aspect. All are important, but here are three which often occur together: The first is the word "Sin" itself. It is a term taken from archery and means "missing the target." Romans 3:23 says, "All have sinned and fall short of the glory of God." As a boy at school I had to learn to shoot. I don't remember whether I ever hit the "bullseye." I often hit one of the rings around it, sometimes the sandbank behind and once a nearby tree! But, whether by an inch or a mile, if I missed the centre I had come short of the required standard. Had I been practicing archery my arrows may sometimes actually have fallen short, failing even to reach the target.

Now God's standard for all of us is called His "glory" which is the blending of His perfect attributes. We see this in the life and character of Jesus of whom it is said, "We have seen His glory... full of grace and truth." [John 1 :14] In the light of this we all fail hopelessly to reach the target.

The term "missing the mark" can also mean "missing the way" when making a journey. We have missed God's way as Isaiah says, "Each of us has turned to his own way," so that, as He says again, "My thoughts are not your thoughts, neither are your ways my ways, declares the Lord." [Isaiah 53:6 and 55:8] We have all gone the wrong way - a way that leads to destruction.

Rebelling Against God

The second word is "Transgression" which we considered in the chapter on reconciliation. It can do with repeating. The word often means "rebellion" which is a far more serious thing. When driving we have to keep to the correct side of the road, and as long as everyone else does the same there are no problems. Sometimes in a thoughtless moment I may stray over the line. That is "transgression" even though I at once come back to my proper lane. If, however, I deliberately cross the line and, worse still, continue to do so, I am guilty of flouting traffic rules. That is "rebellion" against authority.

Sin is not only missing the perfect target of God's moral standard, but breaking the laws He has laid down for our lives whether we do so ignorantly or deliberately. Like the lines in the road, God's rules are there for our safety and well-being and to disobey them is to court disaster, as we saw in the case of Absalom in chapter 7. Rebellion was such a serious thing in the life of Israel, whether it was against parents, rulers or God Himself, because it was so destructive. Our problem is that we all have within us a rebel spirit. Romans 8:7 makes this clear. "The sinful mind is hostile to God. It does not submit to God's law, nor can it do so." So we see that in ourselves we are not only unwilling, but unable to obey God fully. This is how serious is the problem of our sin.

Crookedness

The third word is "Iniquity," which means crookedness. We are told that Lucifer the guardian angel was perfect in all his ways until "iniquity was found in him." [Ezekiel 28:15] He was twisted because of his pride until finally he became the Devil. God made us to be upright and straight, truthful and pure as He Himself is, but sin in many ways twists or perverts what is beautiful in us. For instance, a woman's good gift of home-making can easily become "house pride." A man's interest in sport, or a proper diligence in his daily work, can so take over his life that his wife and children suffer because of his selfish lifestyle. The gift of sex, given to secure family life and enhance an intimate marriage relationship can degenerate into lust and selfishness. Leadership qualities can become a greed for power, while intellectual ability may produce arrogance and the tendency to despise others. These few examples show us how God's image in us becomes distorted by sin.

All this and more, God had to deal with in order to save us, and He does so by removing our sins so that they no longer exist as a barrier between Himself and us. Psalm 103:12 puts it graphically, "As far as the east is from the west, so far has He removed our transgressions from us." So far! Never to be brought back again! That is how effective is the work of the cross.

God's Solution

These three words - sin, transgression and iniquity - are all used by David in Psalms 32 and 51, when he repented. He then speaks about the removal of his sin using three other terms, the first of which is the word "Forgiven." [Psalm 32:1] Forgiveness is a beautiful thing: it is God's action of grace towards sinners. It literally means the "lifting of a load." Sin brings with it a great burden of guilt, of fear, regret and complications of many kinds, as we well know. These become a crushing load like that on the back of the poor sinner in Pilgrim's Progress, who cried out desperately to be set free. Jesus, who was called the "the Lamb of God who takes away the sin of the world," carried our load so that it might be lifted from us. [John 1: 29]

The second word in Psalm 32:1 is "Covered," important because it lies at the heart of the word "atonement" which in Hebrew means "covering." The mercy seat in the Tabernacle literally meant the "cover" because the sacrificial blood sprinkled there each year removed the people's sins from God's sight. Now there are two ways things can be covered over. When I was a boy in South Africa, I once had a holiday on a Dutch farm where the wife boasted of spotless table linen. My mother had warned me against spilling anything, but the inevitable happened! I tipped my teacup slightly and there it was - an ugly brown tea stain on the snowy cloth! As my hostess, Mrs. Uys, didn't notice, I simply moved my cup and saucer so that no one could see the stain and went on with the meal, pretending it wasn't there. It was there however, and when my "covering" was removed, I had to "come clean" about my fault. Mrs. Uys was very kind about it and when the cloth reappeared there was not a sign of the stain to be found. It had not merely been covered, but cleansed, and I did not need to pretend or feel bad about it any more. So it is with our sins. God has a far better way of covering them than we can ever devise. Psalm 51 uses words like "blot out" and "cleanse." God removes the offensive stain of our sin completely so that it is no longer there in His sight. This is the real covering, "the blood of Jesus which cleanses us from all sin. [1 John 1:7]

As the gospel hymn says:

> *What can wash away my stain?*
> *Nothing but the blood of Jesus.*
> *What can make me whole again?*
> *Nothing but the blood of Jesus.*

The third term in Psalm 32 is "does not count against." This has the idea of a debt being cancelled. We have not fulfilled our obligation to God. We owe Him a vast amount. We have withheld our love, our worship, our very selves from Him and He is entitled to charge us with debt, in fact with robbery. [Malachi 3:8] Yet He has provided a way to cancel our debt and free us to live in a right relationship with Himself.

These are three gracious actions of God in His saving love for us sinners. He lifts the load. He covers and cleanses the stain and He cancels the debt we owe. We are released to become the people God intended, so that we may live with Him and serve Him. What relief, what peace, what joy comes when we know these things! But you may ask, how can God do all this for us? The answer is - by the Cross.

The Cross Answers the Problem

When a person stands trial in a court of law for wrong-doing, he is either proved guilty or not guilty. If the former, he will be sentenced. If the latter, he will be acquitted. In God's court, however, we are all guilty, and yet because of the cross, God is able to pronounce us guiltless. This is put clearly in five important phrases in Romans 3:23 and 24: "All have sinned... and are justified... by His grace... through the redemption... by Christ Jesus." At the heart of these phrases is the word "justified" which we might translate "acquitted" or "pronounced not guilty." A person who is justified is either proved not guilty of a misdeed or shown to be right in what he did.

Now we are guilty sinners and God cannot simply say we are innocent, when in fact we are not. And here is a difficulty. In the Old Testament it was strictly laid down in God's law that guilty people were never to be justified so as to be let off their punishment. God said, "I will not acquit the guilty." "He who justifies the wicked or ungodly is an abomination to the Lord." "He who says to the wicked 'you are righteous' shall be cursed and abhorred." [Exodus 23:7; Proverbs 17:15 and 24:24] These are strong words because such a thing was a perversion of justice which God could not allow because He Himself is just.

When we come to the New Testament, however, God appears to reverse His own law because it says that He "justifies the wicked." [Romans 4:5] How can He possibly do this when He is a God of inflexible justice? How demonstrate His justice while justifying the wicked? The answer is given in Romans 3:24 to 26 [A.V.] "Christ Jesus whom God has set forth to be a propitiation to declare His righteousness: that He might be just and the justifier of Him who believes in Jesus." The key here is the word "propitiation," a strong term which means "that which appeases anger" or "wrath" as the Bible calls it. Because God is righteous His reaction to sin must be wrath and if we sinners are to be saved that wrath must be diverted from us to our representative. In sending His Son as a sacrifice for sin, God Himself provided the means of propitiation in Jesus who willingly came to take our place.

So the justice of God has been satisfied, sin has been totally judged in the atoning death of Christ, and at the same time, the love of God is fulfilled because sinners can be forgiven. Jesus the sinless One, has taken the judgment we deserve so that we, the sinful ones, can be declared righteous. God has resolved the dilemma in the Cross.

A Great and Total Work

The sacrifice of Christ is infinitely great because Christ Himself is so great. As Hebrews chapter 1 emphasises, He is greater than prophets or angels, greater than the very universe He created. His work therefore is as mighty as He is and able to take away the sin of the whole world. Why then should you and I fear to bring our own sins to Him in repentance and faith? What a wonderful message this is! Because of Calvary, the load of your guilt can be lifted, the stain of your sin cleansed, the debt of your transgression cancelled and you can be free to live a new life in relationship with God, indwelt and controlled by the Holy Spirit. No wonder Paul writes, "May I never boast except in the cross of our Lord Jesus Christ." And again, "Oh, the depth of the riches of the wisdom and knowledge of God. To Him be glory forever! Amen!" Can you add your "Amen" to that because you know all your sin has been dealt with by the atoning work of Christ? [Gal. 6:14. Rom.11:33, 36.]

THIRTEEN | **The Cross and the Self-Life**

I once heard a simple story about a woman and a spider web. She kept her house neat and clean but was troubled by the web which kept appearing in the corner of a lofty room. She would sweep it away only to find it there again next day. At last her husband said, "You have been dealing with that web for weeks, don't you think it is time we dealt with the spider?" The point of the illustration is that our sinful acts come out of our sinful nature. There is a difference between sins and sin and while God forgives us our sins as we confess them, He has also dealt with their source which is sin itself deeply embedded in our nature. Let us look now at the Cross in relation to our sinful nature.

God's Image Spoiled

To understand this we must see what was God's original design. It says in Genesis 1:27 that He "made man in His own image." We then read that "God formed man from the dust of the ground and breathed into his nostrils the breath of life and man became a living being." [Gen.2:7] The "image" of God was His moral likeness imprinted on our nature so that, indwelt by the Spirit of God and living in obedience and dependence on Him, we could be secure and fulfilled in every way as children of a loving heavenly Father. But as we have already seen, this likeness was damaged by sin so that God was obliged to say His Spirit could no longer remain [or rule] in man because man had become corrupt. [Genesis 6:3] By yielding to the temptation to be "as gods" so as to be free and independent of God, there entered into man a corrupt principle of selfishness which the Bible calls the "flesh." Human nature, created good and beautiful, had now become sinful, twisted from God's original design, a perverted self, producing sinful tendencies and actions.

Expressions of the Flesh

The "Flesh" or sinful human nature is expressed in many ways. Some, such as self-interest, self-will, self-glory and self-righteousness were mentioned in chapter 11, so there is no need to deal with them again. However there are others.

Self-indulgence is one of them. The sinful nature is out to satisfy its own instincts and desires, uncontrolled and without thought for others. This may apply to our eating, drinking, sexual behaviour, use of money or treatment of our fellow men. Self-indulgence may be either sordid or sophisticated, but, whatever form it takes, the Bible calls it "Lust," as Ephesians 2:3 [A.V.] says, "We all had our way of life in times past in the lusts of our flesh, fulfilling the desires of the flesh and of the mind." Someone has defined "lusting" as "wanting what I want and wanting it NOW." Not just sex, but perhaps the latest model in clothes or computers!

Another expression is self-assertiveness in the sense of wanting to dominate. Being rude and aggressive, argumentative and stubborn. Doing all the talking in company, being self-opinionated and "bossy." I used to think this was the sign of strong character, until the Lord showed me it was sin and not like Jesus.

Then there is self-effort. A good thing, you say, and necessary if one is to get on in life. God certainly does not condone laziness. But He cannot bless us if we strive to do things in our own strength without regarding Him at all or admitting that we need Him. This is working "in the flesh" which the Bible says "cannot please God." The works of the flesh, however much they may achieve, are in the end brought to judgment. This is the whole message of the Bible and especially the books of Ecclesiastes and Revelation.

There is also self-pity, a form of the flesh which hides itself away in dark corners. It may seem harmless enough, but it is a corrosive thing which spoils the social atmosphere and makes excessive demands on others.

Doreen and I, when on a journey once in the north of England, started to discuss various problems and soon found ourselves grumbling to one another about everything in general while becoming more and more sorry for ourselves. Presently we came to a village with a name that startled us. There it was on a sign in big letters - "PITY ME." Believe it or not it is on the map! When we saw it, we first began to laugh, then to repent of our self-pity. We asked the Lord's forgiveness and continued happily on our way. I have had to repent many times of this sin of self-centeredness. Always thinking or talking about myself and how situations affect me as though no one else mattered, when all around there are so many crying out for attention and care.

We need to know what God has to deal with in regard to our sinful nature. Why is this so serious? Because it is the very character of God's adversary the Devil who is the essence of selfishness. The "flesh" is offensive to God because it is corrupt. "The old self... corrupted by its deceitful desires." [Ephesians 4:22] It is a violation of His high purpose for mankind, the complete opposite of His nature and the disposition of His Son the Lord Jesus.

The Bible has nothing good to say about the sinful nature. It is "hostile to God, does not submit to God's law and those controlled by it cannot please Him." [Romans 8:7,8] The only thing God can do with the "flesh" is to judge it.

Sinful Nature Condemned in the Cross

In the epistle to the Romans, chapter eight, we are clearly taught that sinful nature is condemned in the cross. In verse three it says that God sent His Son, Jesus, in the likeness of sinful man. He was born as a man, but without any taint of sin or selfishness. Yet at Calvary He took all our sin upon Himself, becoming a sin-offering and so taking the judgment of God on our sinful human nature.

> *Bearing shame and scoffing rude,*
> *In my place condemned He stood.*

That is why Paul in Galatians 2:20 could say, "I have been crucified with Christ." He saw the selfish "I," which lies at the root of all sin, nailed to the Cross and judged in the person of Jesus, our substitute. This was God's full and final verdict on the sinful nature of man with all its corruption and evil effects. The horror of Calvary reveals the depths of our sinful self-life.

Sinful Nature Judged in Our Lives

God has dealt with our self-life in the death of Christ. He now proceeds to deal with it in us, beginning with our conversion when we turn from self and sin to Christ in repentance and faith. Think how radical was the conversion of Paul as he lay broken in the dust on the Damascus road. He had lived a moral and religious life, glorying in everything to do with himself which he considered gave him merit. In Philippians 3:4 he speaks of this as "putting confidence in the flesh." Now, in accepting and acknowledging Jesus as Lord of his life, he turns his back in repentance on all the things that had been "profit" to him in his former way of life, reckoning them "loss" compared with the "surpassing greatness of knowing Christ Jesus." He even considered them rubbish to be thrown away. [see chapter 1, "The Tip"] The Cross had completely changed all his values. Paul then demonstrated this by being baptised. He later taught how, by immersion in water and emergence from it in baptism, we witness to the fact that the old sinful self-life has been buried with Jesus and our new life has risen in His resurrection. [Romans 6: 4-6]

All this wonderful truth has to work out in our daily living. A friend of mine said that when he was baptised he came out of the water "wetter, but no better." He meant by this that more is needed than an outward act, there has to be an inward work. We are told in Romans 6:6 that "our old self was crucified with Christ." This means it has already happened as far as God is concerned. He has written off our self-life in the death of Christ so as to make way for a new life in the Holy Spirit. It is another matter, however, for us to realise this in practice. As one man said, "I know my 'old man' is dead, the trouble is he won't lie down!" Don't we all find this is so, that "self" is very much alive in us? How then do we work out the principle of the cross in our life? How can we consider ourselves dead to sin? I used to have great problems with this truth. I believed what the Bible said that I was "crucified with Christ" and each morning I hoped it would be true that day, so that as Paul said, "I no longer live but Christ lives in me." [Gal. 2:20] Yet however much I tried I would find myself failing before breakfast was over. This "dying to self" seemed impossible. I simply could not make it work. What helped me eventually was this. I had always believed that in the crucifixion Jesus was condemned in my place, but I had not taken seriously enough the fact that the cross was God's condemnation of my sin. In taking Christ as my Saviour I had accepted God's judgment on my sinful self. I now needed to accept this judgment every day in respect of each sin as it came to light. I saw that in repenting I had to judge the sins that God had already judged and put away in the crucifixion of Christ. As a result, repentance began to take on a deeper significance. It was not simply saying "sorry" in a casual way, but seeing the wrong in its true light as something that made it necessary for Christ to die. As a result I had to turn away from it quickly, repudiate it and want never to do it again. How could I condone any sin God had condemned? I must agree with Him and condemn it even as He had. Someone has said, "Repentance is taking sides with God against myself."

It is most important to see repentance as the key to the experience of the cross in our daily living. If we fail to see this, then we are left in frustration, vainly striving to "crucify the flesh" which we are told has already been crucified.

The War Within

Does this mean the end of all conflict? No, because our sinful nature is always in us. It is something like the war between king Saul and David recorded in the book of Samuel. Saul, though rejected by God, refused to give up his kingship. David, however, though chosen by God to be king, did not yet possess the crown. So there was a long war. But we read that "David grew stronger and stronger while the house of Saul grew weaker and weaker" until Saul was finally defeated and David enthroned as king. [2 Samuel 3:1] So it is with us. There is a war between our sinful nature and the Holy Spirit as we are told in Galatians 5:17. But as we persist in repentance, learning in one situation after another how self has to die so as to let Jesus have His way, there will be more of Him and less of us. As John the Baptist said, "He [Christ] must become greater and I must become less." [John 3:30] In this way repentance leads us into holiness and a joy-filled life.

Why is it that sometimes we lack this joy? That even after repenting we sometimes remain sad? The story of Saul and David throws a helpful light on this. After God had been obliged to reject Saul as king, the prophet Samuel who had anointed him spent much of his time in disappointment and sorrow. He had set his hopes on Saul in the beginning. Now those hopes were crushed, his own reputation was tarnished and probably his pride hurt. God eventually spoke to him saying, "How long will you mourn for Saul, since I have rejected him as king? I have chosen one of Jesse's sons to be king." Then later He said, "Arise and anoint him. [David] He is the one. " [1 Samuel 16:1 and 12.]

Are there not times when we find ourselves "mourning for Saul?" Sorrowing over our damaged reputation or the loss of our good opinion of ourselves and of our own righteousness? Mourning over some failure or other when we had expected perfection? "How could I have said this or done that?" we ask ourselves. "How could I have been so stupid or selfish, so weak-willed or bad-tempered?" The answer is that this is how we are. It is the way our self-life behaves. If we are "mourning" it is because we wish it were not so. We cannot accept that "Saul" is a failure, a "write-off" who must be set aside in favour of another. The truth is we are really mourning over ourselves. Are you even now "mourning for Saul?" What are you to do? Accept God's judgment on him. Get up and anoint God's chosen King - Jesus!

Positive Results

The Cross divides between two kinds of life, one defined as "living according to the sinful nature," the other as "living in accordance with the Spirit." We all follow and submit to one or the other. This is clearly explained in Romans 8: 5-11 which tells how the sinful self leads only to spiritual death, but the Holy Spirit brings life and peace with all the blessings that belong to the children of God.

Jesus died to save us from our sins and give us new life. But in 2 Corinthians 5:15 we read that He also died "that they who live should no longer live for themselves, but for Him who died for them and rose again." By His death and resurrection we are released from the bondage of selfishness so that Jesus may be our life-centre, His glory our goal and His Spirit our power. He is to be our All-in-all.

The Cross which to many seems to be negative actually frees us to live in the positive power of the Spirit of God with all His gifts and fruit. We can live a life in which the image of God, so deeply spoiled by sin, is more and more re-created in us until in heaven we are finally made perfect in love. Meanwhile we have to learn to get on with one another both in the church and in our daily life.

FOURTEEN | # The Cross and the Church

We often find a cross in a church building, on a wall, a communion table or even on the rooftop. In this chapter we are not concerned with material crosses, but with the spiritual meaning of the cross of Christ in the life of the church fellowship. Sometimes a church may have fine singing and preaching, good congregations and excellent buildings, yet the Cross may be missing in the experience of the people and the life of the fellowship. There is a little verse I have sometimes quoted -

> *To dwell above with saints we love*
> *Will be eternal glory.*
> *To dwell below with saints we know,*
> *That's quite another story!*

This was the situation in the church to which Paul wrote his first letter to the Corinthians. The fellowship excelled in many things for which Paul commended them. [1 Cor. 1:4-7] They had four major problems however, which he dealt with in the letter. They were: (i) Divisions. (ii) Deterioration of moral behaviour. (iii) Disputes and Difficulties in personal matters. (iv) Disorders in worship.

All these are with us today and, if not dealt with, can cause disastrous results in the witness and even the existence of a church. Paul in addressing these problems shows that the answer to them lies in the principle and power of the cross of Christ. He reminds them that, "When I came to you... I resolved to know nothing while I was with you except Jesus Christ and Him crucified." [1 Cor 2:1,2.] Obviously he had taught many aspects of christian truth, but his basic emphasis had been the atoning death of Christ. It was the foundation of their faith; now it must be the fabric of that faith. They had trusted in it for their salvation; now they needed to experience it in their life together. They believed the doctrine of the atonement but they now had to learn the principle of brokenness which it involved. So in dealing with this divided church Paul, as it were, plants the cross firmly in each of the four situations.

Pride is the Problem

The Cross is the answer to church divisions. This is the theme of chapters 1-4. In 1:10 his appeal is that "all of you agree with one another, so that there may be no divisions among you and that you be perfectly united [joined together] in mind and thought." A 'tall order' as we say! Yet this is what God wants for His people. It is what Jesus prayed for. Why then was this church not being "perfectly united"?

The cause of their divisions was not so much wrong theology as wrong relationships, which is often true in churches today. Paul shows that the divisions had arisen through "contentions." These were caused by jealousies and rivalries springing from selfish pride and conceit, all of which produced foolish boasting. [See 1:12; 3:3 and 21; 4:6 and 18.] Because of this the Corinthian church was split into factions, either boasting in some leader or glorying in spiritual gifts and superior knowledge. Wherever there is this sort of pride there is sure to be criticism, envying and dissension.

Paul shows that the answer to human pride is the cross. This is the thrust of the argument in chapter 1 verses 17-29. The crucifixion of Christ, which was foolishness to the Gentiles and an offence to the Jews, was actually the wisdom and power of God. This is what the

Corinthians did not understand, so instead of their church being ruled by the spirit of Calvary which is humility and sacrifice, it was dominated by worldly pride and self-seeking. It can be the same today.

Where there are tensions and divisions among us, we may be sure pride is at the root. If we glory in our preachers or our premises, our traditions or our triumphs, in anything except the Lord Himself, we sow the seeds of division and decay in the church. "Let him who glories, glory in the Lord," was Paul's counsel to the Corinthians. [1 Corinthians 1:31.] Is he not also saying this to us? He then deals with the second problem.

Closing the Door on Sin

The Cross is the answer to deterioration in moral behaviour. The city of Corinth was a centre of immorality out of which the Christians had been saved. But in chapter five we see how the church condoned an immoral situation which even the pagans would not allow. What is more they were too proud to feel any grief about it. We know how events like this can happen when selfish instincts dictate personal behaviour.

In chapter 5: 6-9 Paul refers to the time when Israel went out of Egypt. A lamb killed and eaten in every family on the passover night marked the end to their old life and the start of their new. This break was symbolised by getting rid of all yeast from their baking dough, eating only unleavened bread that night and starting again with fresh yeast. Paul then says, "Christ our Passover Lamb has been sacrificed," and so we are to get rid of all yeast of wickedness, because through His death we have been brought out of our sinful life to be joined to Him in a new life of holiness, as members of Christ Himself and temples of the Holy Spirit. [Chapter 6: 15-20] Calvary has closed the door on the life of sin and opened another into a life of righteousness. We must therefore "get rid of the old yeast." And that means radical repentance of all unholy actions and attitudes in the light of the sacrifice of Christ our passover Lamb. Our moral behaviour should always be governed by the cross.

Rights and Wrongs

The third issue at Corinth was that of disputes in personal and domestic relationships. These are described in chapters 6-8 and relate to four situations.

For instance there were lawsuits. [6:1-8] Disputes arose between church members often involving personal rights. So they were going to the secular courts even about trivial matters and this was damaging the witness of the church. It showed that the church was defeated because it could not itself settle such problems. Paul says to each member, "Why not rather be wronged?" "Impossible!" we say. But Jesus was wronged when He went to the Cross, yet by committing Himself to God His Father He emerged victorious.

Then there were marital problems. [chapter 7] These were complicated matters, as they still are today. Should one marry or stay single? Should couples stay together if they do not share the same faith? What about mutual responsibilities and rights? All these Paul treats at length, but at the heart of his counsel is the principle of the cross which comes through everything he says, such as, "Do not deprive each other." "Each should retain the place in life God has assigned to him." He tells couples that they belong to one another in such a way that each is to be committed to the other's good. Can you see in the submission, sacrifice, surrender of rights, and mutual love, the working out of the principle of the cross? [See 7: 16,17] What a difference it makes in our homes and marriages when Jesus is Lord and Calvary is the principle that governs our life together.

The Strong and the Weak

Next there were uncertain matters of conscience which occupy chapters 8 to 10. The main problem for the church was that of eating food which had been offered to idols. Such an offering was a religious ritual and the food was then sold in the market. Some felt they had a right to eat since for them the idols had no spiritual reality. Others were convinced idols had to do with evil powers, so the food was tainted and must not be touched. A thorny problem indeed! Paul again applies the principle of the cross. Let those who felt free to eat consider those who felt condemned if they ate. Let the "strong" brother consider how his action would affect the "weak" brother for whom Christ had died.

Since Christ the strong Son of God gave up His rights and His freedom in order to die for helpless sinners, should we not give up our rights for one another? This was the principle of Paul's whole life - the principle of the cross. Today we have other kinds of uncertain issues of conscience in which each one must decide what he should do without passing judgment on others. Yet all must be done in the light of Calvary. And that may mean letting go our rights for the sake of another whose sensitive conscience might be hurt by our action. This is the way of love which produces a wholesome and helpful church where each one surrenders all that is selfish at the feet of the Saviour.

Love is the Answer

The last area of concern for Paul in the Corinthian church was that of difficulties arising in their worship and the exercise of spiritual gifts. These are dealt with in chapters 11 to 14. Because of unruly conduct at the Lord's Table, and confusion in the use of "charismatic" gifts, many problems existed which came about through selfishness, vanity and lack of love. In my christian life I regret to say that from time to time I have witnessed such situations with all the harm they produced.

The answer again is the Cross. At the Communion we "proclaim the Lord's death." In the breaking of the bread and the pouring of the wine we set forth vividly the suffering and self-giving of our Saviour, and it is a serious matter if we do not "recognise the body of the Lord," or we "eat the bread and drink the cup of the Lord in an unworthy manner." [11:26-29] There is no place for greed, selfishness, or frivolous behaviour of any kind, among those who gather round the Lord's Table. There was none of this in Jesus.

Similarly, spiritual gifts which Paul deals with in chapters 12 and 14 should be exercised in the light and the spirit of Calvary. We are to use them not for self-satisfaction, but for the good of others and in subjection to the Holy Spirit and to one another. Above all, they must be governed and permeated by love. This is the great theme of chapter 13. Someone I knew always insisted on reading the word love as "Calvary love." It is the love of Christ so evident in His life and finally in His sacrifice. Not sentimental love, but that which is practical and self-giving to others. We can only realise and reveal that love as we live together at the cross where pride is humbled, sin repented of, rights surrendered, disputes settled, divisions healed, fellowship deepened, worship made pure and the glory of God shown in the life of the church.

Snakes in the Sand

Only as the Cross [not only in its evangelical, but also its moral sense] is central in the church can these problems be solved. Let me illustrate how this can happen.

In the book of Numbers chapter 21 we read of a time when in the desert, the people of Israel, because of their sinfulness, were plagued by an invasion of "venomous snakes" which bit them so that many died. God did not take these deadly creatures away and there seemed no solution. Except one!

A great bronze snake was made at God's command and lifted up on a pole so that everyone could see it. Whoever was bitten had only to look at it in obedience to God and be healed. The snakes never gained the upper hand because the camp was dominated by God's remedy. The Lord Jesus, in John 3:15, used this incident to show that He was to be "lifted up" so that all who looked to Him in faith would have spiritual healing and new life. He later spoke several times of the cross in terms of His being "lifted up." We know we are saved initially by "looking" in faith to the Saviour, but we need to be saved continually in the same way. The "snakes" are with us still, not lurking in the sands of Sinai, but hiding in situations in the church fellowship. We have mentioned some of them and there are many more. They will always be with us, but they need not do harm or gain control if in repentance and faith we constantly look to Calvary where the snake venom has already been drawn. The church that lives in the light of the Cross will live in the life of the Spirit in spite of the "snakes."

What kind of fellowship will be produced where we are willing to bind every problem back to the cross as Paul encouraged the Corinthian church to do? And what sort of Christians will be part of such a church? Let us look at this in the next chapter.

FIFTEEN | # The Servant Heart

Let us go back to the few days before Jesus was to die at Calvary. His enemies were plotting to kill Him and one of His followers had planned to betray Him. Other disciples were arguing among themselves as to who was to be the greatest. In this atmosphere of rivalry, apprehension and mistrust they were sitting together at a meal, when He who was far greater than all of them left His place at the head of the table, took off His outer clothes, wrapped a towel around Him, filled a bowl with water, then knelt down in front of His disciples and humbly washed their feet. Jesus, God's Son, their Saviour and Master was demonstrating the full extent of His love for them.

Public footwashing is foreign to our culture. But in that time and climate where days were hot, roads dusty and sandals the general footwear, people were always washing their feet. If you were wealthy it was done for you and your visitors by slaves. And the lowest rank of slaves at that. [See John 13: 1-17 and Philippians 2: 1-8] It must have felt good to have your feet washed after walking through the dust - clean, fresh and fit for the company of others.

Jesus at the Feet of Sinners

What a picture we have here! Jesus at the feet of sinners! Knowing that He had come from God, was going back to God and had been given control of all things by God, Jesus kneels to wash His disciples' feet. His origin, status and destiny are the very highest. Yet He stoops to wash dirty feet. There are only two words to describe such an action - "marvellous grace"! Slaves had no authority, no liberty, no rights. Jesus took this powerless place, performing the task of the lowest slave. In doing this He was acting out symbolically the drama of His saving love for sinners which we read about in Philippians chapter 2. There He is shown putting aside His heavenly splendour to take human nature, then to become a humble servant among us and pour out His own sinless life-blood on the cross to provide cleansing for our sins. Peter did not like what Jesus was doing. So he protested, only to be told, "Unless I wash you, you have no part with me." It was a salutary warning! We can have no fellowship with the Lord nor share in His kingdom unless He removes our sin. For us, then, cleansing is essential. Furthermore it must be continual. When we first believe we are, as it were, bathed completely, justified by faith, totally accepted and made clean in God's sight. But sin, still in our nature, surfaces at many points - in our looks, tones, actions, reactions and in many a slip and fall. Have you not found it so? I certainly have. As we walk the Christian way our "feet" get soiled. It is no use covering them up. They must be exposed to Jesus in repentance and confession whenever it is needed. Then His blood will keep on cleansing us from sin so that we may continue in fellowship with Him. [1 John 1:7]

The action of Jesus described in John 13 shows us His attitude and disposition to be that of a servant, something which does not come naturally to me. The Son of God came not to be served but to serve; I, on the other hand, so often like to be honoured and served. How different! I need constantly to learn the meaning of grace - God coming down to reach and cleanse me at my many points of defilement; Jesus at my feet when I should be at His!

Sinners at the Feet of Jesus

Over against this event we read of another, in Luke 7:37-39, where we find a sinner at the feet of Jesus. An immoral woman, hearing that He was eating in a Pharisee's home, came and knelt before Jesus, weeping so much that her tears washed His feet. She then dried them with her long hair, kissed them and finally poured a jar of perfume on them. In her tears I see the symbol of her repentance, in the act of drying the Lord's feet is her acceptance of pardon, her kisses speak of gratitude and devotion, while the anointing shows her recognition of Jesus as her Messiah. All this because she so greatly loved the One who had forgiven her so much. Surely when we see how Jesus has stooped to wash our feet, we will want to wash His? But how different are these feet. Ours have walked in the ways of selfishness, His in the paths of obedience and devotion. In soiling our feet we have pierced His, and when we touch His feet we touch the wounds our sins have made. Then it is we must say with Charles Wesley:

> *O let me kiss your wounded feet,*
> *and bathe and wash them with my tears!*
> *The story of your love repeat*
> *in every drooping sinner's ears;*
> *That all may hear the quickening sound,*
> *since I, even I, have mercy found.*

Those who often come to Jesus to be washed will not only be found washing His feet, but will long to lead others into the same experience.

Washing One Another's Feet

Jesus washing the feet of sinners reveals His grace. Sinners washing His feet shows their repentance and devotion. Yet the picture is still not complete. We need to wash one another's feet. This is fellowship. The Lord said, "I have set you an example that you should do as I have done. You should wash one another's feet." Whether this was meant literally we don't know. Actual footwashing has been practiced through the ages and still is by the Mennonite churches. In a moving and meaningful service their leaders and members kneel humbly to wash one another's feet, sharing their needs, confessing their faults while praying for one another. Usually, however, we regard the Lord's words in a spiritual sense. So what does it mean?

First, we must relate to one another as those who need their feet washed, that is as sinners, willing to be known not as perfect people, but as those who fail and often need to repent and be cleansed. Each disciple by uncovering His feet to Jesus, in the same act disclosed them to the others. Only as we recognise one another as sinners can we truly know one another as brothers. Then as we do this, we will help each other to repent. Often I am not willing or quick to repent. Perhaps I do not recognise my fault and need the faithful challenge of someone else to show me where I am wrong and point me to the cleansing blood of Jesus.

At one time when I lived under a great sense of guilt a brother wrote to me saying, "Stanley, you are only seeing your sinfulness. You need to see the blood of Christ which is infinitely greater than all your sin." I owe a lot to that faithful counsel. It set me free from condemnation and brought me into the joy of continual forgiveness.

We also need to forgive others and ask them to forgive us. Unless we do so, our feet will remain soiled and we will not be free. The dust of resentment and the odour of bitterness will cling to them. They may become hardened and even diseased. There is nothing so corrosive as an unforgiving spirit, nothing so damaging to our fellowship with the Lord and one another. Do you need to come with anyone else at this time to wash at the place of forgiveness? This means submitting to each other in humble love, something we may find hard to do. Yet Jesus knelt before His disciples, the woman bowed before Him, and we need to bend in submission to one another. What a difference there is in the home and the church when we do this!

It is like the crossroads where the signs say, "Give way" or "Yield," and as each driver in turn does so, the traffic flows safely and smoothly. We see this sign before us as we see Jesus giving up His rights on the cross. Then the Spirit will teach us where we need to "yield" and so learn the meaning of "brokenness" in our homes and churches. [Ephesians 5:21]

Real fellowship involves our serving one another in love, not feeling ashamed to take the powerless place or do some menial task. I was touched when I once saw a church pastor after conducting a service in a most able manner, pick up a broom and sweep an untidy floor in a hall where his congregation had taken refreshments. Here was a leader willing to be a servant. And seeing him I saw Jesus.

There is more to it than this. To serve one another in love is to care; to touch the needs of others wherever we discern them. It is to consider, console, encourage, exhort one another as we are able. It is to share testimony, impart truth so as to edify others and leave them helped, uplifted and encouraged. Footwashing not only means cleansing but refreshing so that we have a spring in our step as we go on our way together.

Doreen told me how once at Christmas she found herself working hard on her own in the kitchen from where she could hear laughter and lively talking going on in the living room. Gradually she became full of resentment and self-pity so that all the joy she had known in preparing for the "family day" ebbed away as she began to blame others for their thoughtlessness. At that moment she picked up a card which had just arrived in the post. It was a famous picture of Jesus washing His disciples' feet. Seeing Him serving with bowed head at the feet of sinners was challenge enough to help her to repent and find her joy restored. "Lord Jesus give me your servant heart! Create in me the spirit of the Lamb who came to give Himself for me on the cross of Calvary."

SIXTEEN | # Where is the Lamb?

Children often ask their parents questions which are difficult or impossible to answer. One day a lad called Isaac asked his father an awkward question - "Where is the lamb for the burnt offering?" [Genesis 22:7] Abraham had been told by God to offer Isaac, his only son, as a burnt offering on a mountain called Moriah. This was only intended to test his faith and obedience because God was going to provide the sacrifice in His own way. Father and son were now on their way with both wood and fire for the sacrifice. But no lamb! So we can understand Isaac's question.

The Importance of the Lamb

Three things were needed for the Jewish burnt offering - wood, fire and an animal for sacrifice, which could be a bullock, sheep or goat, but the most common was a lamb.

A sacrificial lamb was required to have three qualities: First purity. It had to be free from all blemishes or defects. Second humility. Unlike some animals, lambs were meek creatures. Isaiah wrote "He is led like a lamb to the slaughter, as a sheep dumb before her shearers is silent, so He did not open His mouth." [Isaiah 53:7] The third factor was sacrifice, for which the lamb was set apart.

In each of these qualities the lambs on Jewish altars typified Christ who in John 1:36 was called "The Lamb of God." He was sinless and spotless, the only perfect man who has ever lived. And although He was the mighty Son of God, He was "meek and lowly in heart," always willing to minister to others and eventually to die as a sacrifice for our sins.

Jesus - God's Perfect Lamb

A lamb for a burnt offering was first killed, then all its blood poured out near to an altar on which finally the body was burnt. As the smoke rose up it represented the total dedication of the worshipper to God. The sacrifice is described in Leviticus 1: 9, 13, 17, as "an aroma pleasing to the Lord," not because of the smell of roasting meat, but what it represented. In the New Testament we are told that it foreshadowed the sacrifice of God's Son, who would offer Himself in perfect love "as a fragrant offering and sacrifice to God." [Ephesians 5:2] Jesus is our great "burnt offering" who gave Himself up for us as "a lamb without blemish or defect," having humbled Himself to die on a cross. [1 Peter 1:19, Phil.2:8] He was God's perfect lamb and throughout the last book of the Bible, Revelation, Jesus is continually called "The Lamb."

Yet it was not only in the sacrifice of lambs that God saw Christ the heavenly Lamb, but in the spirit of the lamb in people. He saw it in Abraham's obedience, in Moses' meekness, in David's humility, in Jeremiah's sorrow over the sins of the people and in Hosea's sacrificial love for his profligate wife. God responded to the Christlike attitude He saw in them and He looks for this spirit in us and in our churches. Isaac's question is still God's question to us today, "Where is the Lamb?"

God's Important Question

God can often say "Here is the wood," carefully laid out in our systematic doctrines, precise programmes and "orders of service," all of which can be dry, hard and dead. Or He may have to say, "Here is the fire, plenty of fervour, excitement and lively worship, sometimes to the detriment of the "wood"! All too often we set the one against the other even to the point of conflict and division, but the fact is we need to hold both in balance - order with freedom, zeal with truth, and all as means to exalt Jesus the Lamb. What matters is how important and central He is in us personally and in our churches. Neither the wood nor the fire can burn without the other: both are needed but only as they exist for the lamb. God is still saying, "Where is the lamb?"

Abraham was unable to provide the lamb. Neither can we. It is not in us to produce the purity, humility and sacrificial love God requires. But Abraham discovered God already had a lamb prepared for him. That is why he called the place "Jehovah Jireh" - the Lord will provide. Not provide anything he might ask for, but what was essential - the lamb! We must remember that our basic need is atonement for sin. We may have riches, health and much else we think necessary and God gives these as He sees fit. Our deepest need, however, is to be forgiven and saved from our sins and this Jesus alone can supply because He is the Lamb. He always was the Lamb, both in heaven before the creation of the world and on earth as He lived to obey His Father and then at Calvary where He gave Himself in sacrifice for our sins.

The fact is that Jesus is all we are not. None of us qualify before God as spotless, lowly, self-sacrificing lambs. Far from it. But Jesus does. He perfectly satisfies God and so provides what we cannot offer. What then are we to do? Try to be like Him? In ourselves we never will. What we can do and must do is to admit where we are not the lamb and come to the one who is. This is what a man did in Israel when he brought his sacrifice to God. We read that he had to "Lay his hand on the head of the offering" so that it "would be accepted instead of him to make atonement on his behalf that he might be accepted before the Lord." As an imperfect sinner he could only be acceptable to God in his substitute, the perfect lamb offered in his place.[Leviticus 1:3,4; 3: 7,8 and 4:33] This is how we first become Christians and how we should go on.

Working It Out in Practice

Many years ago when our family was young and at home, I remember a morning when everything seemed to go wrong. None of us was very sweet-tempered and I for one was irritable and harsh. Every day after breakfast, we each read a Bible verse from a little book before we prayed. That day the theme was the Lamb. When I came to read my verse it said, "Isaac said to his father 'where is the lamb?'" As I paused for thought, someone murmured, "Not around here this morning!" Another verse was "He shall lay his hand on the head of the lamb." I saw how unlike Jesus I had been and often was, and as we prayed I had to confess my bad temper and pride, and in repentance "lay my hand" on Jesus to receive forgiveness. Others did the same and everything was changed. Jesus the Lamb was there with us all the time. We had only to come to Him. And we still do.

We know that the ground of salvation is not our imperfect works, but the perfect atoning work of Christ. It is also the way of peace and holiness. Not by striving to be like the Lamb, but admitting where we are not. Then as we turn to Jesus in repentance and faith we find not only that He is all we can never be, but that we are accepted and made holy in Him.[Eph.1:6,4] As we walk with Him He enables us to share His perfect lamb-like nature. The cross is also the ground of our fellowship with God and with one another as we gather round the Lamb - sinners willing to lose our self-righteousness on this matter and that, and to forgive one another as we live in the forgiveness of the Lord. Then the Holy Spirit fills us, love flows in our hearts and we have true fellowship. But only as we all lay our hands on the head of the Lamb and say again,

> *Just as I am without one plea,*
> *But that thy blood was shed for me,*
> *And that thou bid'st me come to thee,*
> *O Lamb of God I come.*

But you ask "Is not all this very negative?" No, exactly the opposite. It is God's way of peace, joy, holiness and victory. Where Jesus the Lamb is, there is every blessing. Satan is defeated, for it says, "The Lamb shall overcome" and those who walk with Him share in His victory. [Revelation 17:14] The Lamb is victorious because by His death on the Cross for our sins He has taken away Satan's ground in us and in this way stripped him of his power. He has triumphed over all the evil powers in His Cross and sealed His conquest in the resurrection. The victory of Jesus is our victory as well. That is why it says, "They overcame him [Satan] by the blood of the Lamb." [Revelation 12:11]

The Lamb in the Throne

Where then is the Lamb? He is in the throne of God as the book of Revelation tells us. He is King of kings and Lord of lords, yet He is still the Lamb, pure, gentle and scarred with the marks of Calvary. He is also in the church by the presence of the Holy Spirit in the heart and life of every believer. Christ is in us as the Lord to whom we must submit, but also as the Lamb who is our Saviour and our example. Our need will often be for forgiveness as we see where we are not pure and gentle like Him. Then as we turn to Him in repentance we can thank Him again that He is not only our example, but our perfect sacrifice and our source of spiritual life and power. We shall see in the next chapter something more of the victory of the Lamb.

SEVENTEEN | The Victory of the Lamb

The last book in the Bible, Revelation, is not easy to understand. It is full of visions, symbolic figures and mysterious events. However, through all of these strange pictures one message comes through, - the triumph of the Lord Jesus Christ over all the forces of evil. It is summed up in the phrase, "The Lamb will overcome, because He is Lord of lords and King of kings." [Rev. 17:14]

All through the book, Jesus is called "The Lamb" whose triumph is described in the fifth chapter. John the writer has a vision of God on His throne holding in His right hand a sealed scroll in which are written all His judgments and purposes. No-one is able to look into this scroll, nor is worthy to open it except "The Lion of the tribe of Judah," the only one who "has triumphed." You would expect a lion, the king of the beasts to overcome, would you not? However, when John looks for this great "lion," he sees instead a little lamb, " looking as though it had been slain." Yet it is this pathetic looking lamb who takes the scroll and opens it. Then a great song goes up in heaven, "You are worthy to take the scroll and open its seals, because You were slain, and by Your blood have purchased men for God from every tribe and language and people and nation... and they will reign on the earth." [Rev. 5:9,10] What a sight and what a song!

Jesus who was crucified is alone qualified to handle the great purposes of God not only in redemption, but also in judgment. There are awesome pictures of judgment in Revelation chapter 6 as the Lamb opens the seals of the scroll until eventually, amid violent cosmic disturbances, men everywhere fly in terror, crying out to be hidden from the face of God and from "the wrath of the Lamb." Those who have not hidden in Jesus in the day of His grace will run to hide from Him in the day of His wrath. He who is the Saviour of sinners is also the one whose blazing righteousness will consume everything that is evil.

Jesus, Always Victorious

Jesus "the Lion" triumphed because He was the Lamb. So the book of Revelation calls Him the Lamb twenty seven times, always as one who is victorious. Victory was the pattern of His life. He who had come among men to be the Lamb of God, surprised the doctors of the law by His questions as a boy and amazed His hearers by His wisdom as a man. Jesus always prevailed. We can see this specially in the records of Luke's gospel. For instance He overcame when tempted by the Devil. [4:13] He had authority in speaking and teaching. [4:32] He conquered demon powers, healed sicknesses and handled insoluble problems. [4:36-41; 5:4-6; 9:10-17] He had mastery over people [5:27 and 20:26] and finally was given authority over all things. [22:69 and Matthew 28:18] So you see Jesus was always Master and Lord. When He came to Calvary, however, He was willing to be weak and powerless, refusing to "come down from the Cross." He was "crucified in weakness," [2 Corinthians 13:4] dying not as the mighty lion, but as the helpless lamb.

Yet the cross which seemed His ultimate defeat was in fact His final victory. His last cry was not "I am finished," but "It is finished" - *tetelestai* in the original Greek text, which was often shouted by Roman armies to announce their triumph in battle. In His victorious cry Jesus was proclaiming that His great work of atonement for sinners was completed.

Jesus, Victorious in the Cross

How then was this victory achieved? The answer is given in Colossians 2: 14,15. "He forgave us all our sins, having cancelled the written code with its regulations that was against us; He took it away, nailing it to His cross. And having disarmed the powers and authorities He made a public spectacle of them, triumphing over them by the cross." The "written code" was the law of God which could only condemn us because we fail to keep it. It is a debt we cannot pay. We are told that in olden times, creditors would nail up for public display the receipts for amounts paid by their debtors so that everybody would know the debts had been settled. So Christ being nailed to the cross meant the debt we owed to God was nailed there in His crucified body showing it had been paid.

The "powers and authorities" refer not so much to the Romans and Jews as to the powers of wickedness - Satan and his whole evil empire to which we are in bondage through our sin. Not only are we debtors who cannot pay: we are slaves who cannot escape. Jesus by His death on the cross has dealt with both of these situations. He has settled our debts and severed our bonds. We can be free both from sin's condemnation and Satan's control.

I believe this is what is meant when it says in Revelation 1:5, "To Him who loved us and freed us from our sins by His blood and has made us to be a kingdom and priests to serve His God and Father." And again in 12:11, "They overcame by the blood of the Lamb." The key to both freedom from condemnation and victory over all evil powers is in the blood of Christ which we have already emphasised means His sacrificial death. By atoning for sin, Satan's ground of control has been taken away. We read "that by His death He might destroy him who holds the power of death, that is the Devil, and free those who all their lives were held in slavery." [Hebrews 2:14] In this context the word "destroy" does not mean "annihilate" but "make powerless." As Wesley put it:

> *The reign of sin and death is o'er,*
> *And all may live from sin set free.*
> *Satan has lost his mortal power;*
> *'Tis swallowed up in victory.*

Words you can sing with a "Hallelujah!" in your heart!

Victory Through the Blood

The victory of the cross was won by the power of the blood of Christ, by which He Himself was freed from the burden and condemnation of our sin to rise from the dead and go back into heaven. [Heb. 13:20 and 9:12] If He who was our sinbearer was set free by the power of His own blood, [that is His sacrificed life] then surely we the sinners can be free from sin's condemnation if we belong to Him. The teaching of Scripture is that the blood of Christ was shed to atone for sin, not to protect from accidents or heal from sicknesses. We should never use the blood as a formula to work wonders when ever we mention it, nor should we "claim the blood" for all kinds of needs in our lives. The blood of Christ was shed to atone for sin and cleanse our heart and conscience so that our relationship with God is right and on this basis all our other needs can be taken care of by the Holy Spirit who heals and delivers.

The victory of the cross was sealed by the resurrection and the ascension of our Lord Jesus, who, "after He had provided purification for sins, sat down at the right hand of the Majesty in heaven." [Heb. 1:3] He is "seated in heavenly realms far above all rule and authority, power and dominion and every title that can be given, not only in the present age but also in the one to come." [Eph. 1:20,21] There cannot be any greater victory than this. The triumph of Christ is total and will be made evident when He appears at His second coming. Surely this puts heart and hope into us! In every circumstance we can live in victory because Jesus does. This is the message of Revelation for us today. We must remember it is as the "Lamb" that Jesus overcame.

There is a passage of scripture which I find deeply moving. It is 1 Corinthians 15: 24-28, where we read how at the end of history, when Jesus has destroyed all evil powers and everything is "put under Him," He does not claim anything for Himself, but hands over the kingdom to His Father, so that "God may be all in all." Though He reigns in the throne with His Father, He does so as the Lamb with the lowly spirit. Even in His heavenly glory He still has the Cross in His heart.

"The Lamb shall overcome," is the message of the final book of the Bible. But Jesus also has this promise for us who belong to Him: "To him who overcomes I give the right to sit with me on my throne, just as I overcame and sat down with my Father on His throne." [Rev. 3:21] What an amazing promise! But we must remember that He overcame as the Lamb and only as we follow Him sharing and showing His gentle, loving nature, shall we overcome and share in His victory and authority.

EIGHTEEN

The Final Breakthrough

Reading an old book one day, I came across a strange quotation, "The Breaker is come up." I wonder what you would make of that? I had no idea what it meant or where it had come from, but hazarding a guess it might be in the Bible, I searched my concordance and found it in the book of Micah, chapter 2 and verse 13. When I read it in the New International Version it made more sense to me: "one who breaks open the way will go up before them; they will break through the gate and go out. Their king will pass through before them, the Lord at their head." As I studied the passage, I found it referred to the Messiah coming to break down a wall behind which Israel would be penned in like a flock of sheep. Interesting, because the Jewish people have so often been in such a situation as indeed they are today and will be until their Messiah comes to liberate them.

The Messiah of the Old Testament is the Christ of the New who has come to break down every wall that keeps us from freedom and fullness of life. Not only for the people of Israel, but for all men. And this He has done by His death on the cross. He who came from heaven has, by His sacrifice for our sins, broken open ways where once there were only walls.

The Barrier to Heaven

For one thing, Jesus has broken open the way to God the Father. Charles Wesley wrote:

> *Accepted in the Wellbeloved,*
> *and clothed in righteousness divine;*
> *I see the bar of heaven removed,*
> *and all thy merits Lord are mine.*

What was the "bar to heaven" Wesley saw? It was the barrier between us and God caused by our sin.

In the Jewish Tabernacle, and later in the Temple in Jerusalem, there hung a thick curtain screening the way into the Holy of Holies where God showed His presence in shining light. So awesome was this place that only the High Priest could enter it once a year and then only with the blood of sin offerings. For anyone else to enter would mean death, so serious was the barrier of sin separating men from God.

Jesus was the only one who could deal with this barrier, and He did so by His atoning death; as the hymn says,

> *There was none other good enough*
> *To pay the price of sin;*
> *He only could unlock the gate*
> *Of heaven and let us in.*

We read in the New Testament that when Jesus died, the curtain in the Temple was torn in two, showing that the way to God was open for any sinner who would repent and believe the Gospel. Jesus had come from the glory of heaven to be a sacrifice for our sins. During His earthy life He had always lived in the presence of God, yet on the cross He cried out, "My God, why have you forsaken me?" In that terrible moment He experienced utter separation from His heavenly Father as He took on Himself our sins and their penalty. Yet so effective was His sacrifice in putting away those sins that "the bar to heaven was removed" and He was able to rise from the grave to return to heaven, not for Himself alone, but on behalf of all who trust Him. This is the message of

Hebrews 6: 19, 20. Jesus is our "Forerunner" who has "broken open the way and gone up before," so that where He has gone we too may enter. As Christopher Wordsworth wrote:

> *Mighty Lord in your ascension,*
> *We, by faith, behold our own.*

How important it is to know this great truth and accept by faith that the way to God is open for sinners like us. To believe the fact that Jesus has "entered the Holiest by His own blood, having obtained eternal redemption for us," so that we can "have confidence to enter the Holiest, with full assurance of faith" by this same atoning blood. [Heb.9:12, 24. 10:19,20] As you read these verses, make sure of your place within the curtain torn apart for you at Calvary. Then if, because of some sin or failure, some accusation of the Devil or your own conscience, you feel there is a barrier between you and the Lord, take hold of the fact that "the bar to heaven" has been removed at the Cross. You can enter into freedom, knowing that as you repent and believe, the blood of Jesus is able to bring you as near to God as Jesus is Himself. There is no need for you to remain "penned in" by guilt, fear, vain regrets or any sense of alienation from your heavenly Father.

Barriers Between One Another

There is however another aspect to this. Sin has not only made a barrier between us and God, but walls between us and our fellow men. Yet the Lord Jesus has broken open the way for us to be reconciled. I have dealt with this more fully in chapter 7. Just think of the fearful walls of hostility and hatred between people today, caused by misunderstanding, fear, resentment and jealousy. Any one of these may start very small like fine gauze, hardly noticeable, yet if we allow it to remain it will thicken to become like wire netting. If still left, it becomes a brick wall and finally steel fencing. The remedy for this is that Jesus died to break down every "dividing wall" separating men from one another. [Eph. 2:14] The same sacrificial work that opens the way to God, opens the way to our fellow men because in both cases it is sin that is the barrier. All that alienates us from each other whether in marriage, family or church fellowship, can be removed by the power of the blood of Christ if we are willing to repent, forgive and avail ourselves of God's remedy. It is best to come to Him while our separation is like fine gauze and not wait until it has become steel fencing.

Barriers in Life's Way

What about conditions in our lives? Our way so often appears uncertain, even blocked, so that we are confused and distressed. But Jesus is able to break down barriers in the present and open gates into the future. What is your situation as you read this? Is your marriage or family life a disappointment? Have you lost your job? Is your business or your health under threat? Are you troubled about the present or fearful about the future like the disciples were when Jesus was crucified? Fearful, futureless men; hopeless, heartbroken women. Everything they had believed and hoped for lying in ruins! Yet the cross that seemed the end of their hopes was actually God's "door of hope." A message was given to them, "Do not fear, He is risen and is going before you into Galilee. You will see Him there." For Jesus, the crucifixion which was the end of His earthly life was the way into resurrection life. He Himself had said that after His death He would go before them. And this promise is for all of us. Jesus goes before us into our future for He says, "I am the Living One; I was dead and behold I am alive for ever and ever! And I hold the keys of death and Hades." [Rev. 1: 18]

He who has the keys of death also has the keys of life. As we face our tomorrows He is already there to meet us. The eternal Christ, who came to die in time, has risen the timeless one, Lord of the future, to be our Shepherd, Forerunner, Provider and Guide. The problems we struggle with He has already solved. The situations we face, both in life and death, our Saviour has already entered because He is risen from the dead. As Jim Elliott, missionary to the Auca Indians, said, "I do not know what the future holds, but I know Who holds the future." Can you say the same with the confidence that comes from faith in God?

Breakthrough into the World

Finally, there is the world situation, filled with alternating hope and despair. Shot through at times with bright rays only to be darkened again by doom-laden clouds. What can we make of it? Abandon it to its fate while we wait for the final holocaust? Retreat into our safe haven of spiritual contentment? Not so our Lord Jesus! Having died on the cross for the world, He rose again to be its Saviour. As for His ascension, it was no glad escape from the sorrows of earth into the security of heaven. His last words were, "All authority in heaven and on earth has been given to me. Therefore go and make disciples of all nations." [Matthew 28: 18,19] Then He added, "And surely I am with you always even to the very end of the age." [v.20] By His death He had broken the power of sin and Satan, death and hell and proved it by His resurrection and ascension. Now He promises to go with His people as they take the message of His victory into the world. This was the faith of the first Christians as they went out with the Gospel. It was the vision of the apostle John when he saw the Lord Jesus as an armed rider on a white horse going out to conquer, the sword of God's Word in His hand and the armies of heaven following Him. What a picture of the power of the Gospel to judge and to save as it is preached throughout the earth to the very end of time. [Rev. 19: 11-16]

There are many barriers raised against the kingdom of Christ today, but He is able to break through wherever the cross is proclaimed in the power of the Holy Spirit. It was so in the days of the apostles and is the same in our day as we have seen during this century. Situations that once seemed impossible have opened up to the

Gospel in Africa, China, Eastern Europe, Latin America, Nepal, Russia and many other areas where the Spirit of God is at work.

He is breaking down the barriers, He is casting up the way,
He is calling for His angels to build up the gates of day.
But His angels here are human, not the shining hosts above,
And the drumbeats of His army are the heartbeats of our love.

We live in a world walled in by spiritual darkness, at times seeming impervious to the Gospel light. But He who has broken through all other barriers will also break through this one. In Matthew 11:12 [N.I.V.] we find a strange statement of Jesus - "From the days of John the Baptist until now, the kingdom of heaven has been forcefully advancing, and forceful men lay hold of it." Some scholars associate this verse with the words of Micah 2:13 with which we began this chapter.

During the four hundred years from Malachi to Matthew, there had been no prophets, no fresh revelation of truth and no apparent growth of God's kingdom. Nothing but upheavals and wars. Then suddenly John the Baptist appeared, preaching and bringing crowds to repentance, and at once the kingdom of God began to advance. At the same time, Jesus came, and as He taught, healed and cast out evil spirits, the advance went on throughout His life. With His death on the cross, His resurrection and the sending of the Holy Spirit, there came the greatest breakthrough of the kingdom as men everywhere laid hold of it. From that time on, God's kingdom has grown, sometimes receding only to break out again and again in reformations, revivals and fresh revelations of truth. The progress of Christ's kingdom will continue to the end of time, because nothing can destroy the work of His Cross.

There is a story of a Swiss hero, Arnold von Winkelried, who when his little army was faced with a formidable array of Austrian spear men, rushed ahead of his soldiers and gathering as many of the enemy spears as he could in his wide opened arms, plunged them into his body to make a gap in the opposing ranks through which his men poured and won the battle. Dora Greenwell, in one of her writings, says:

When were Love's arms stretched so wide as upon the Cross?
When did they embrace so much as when Thou, O Christ,
didst gather within Thy bosom the spears and arrows of
the mighty, to open us a lane of freedom?

By taking our sins in His body on the Cross, Jesus breached the ranks of Satan's army. By His death and resurrection He has opened the way into the world so that men everywhere might be reached with the Gospel. He is calling us to "break through the gate and go out" where He leads, as it says in Micah 2:13, "Their king shall pass through before them, the Lord at their head." What a thrilling prospect! What unspeakable privilege and opportunity! He who passed through the darkness of Calvary and has gone before us into the light of heaven, now goes to take that light wherever there is ignorance, error and evil on the earth.

We are to follow where He leads, breaking through every barrier that holds us back. Whether in vision, prayer or evangelism, as well as in our ordinary contacts with others, let us go with our Lord, the great "Breaker of Barriers," and share in the victory of His Cross, the Door of Hope.

On 4th December 1997, Stanley Voke left the land of the dying for the land of the living, to finally see face to face the wonderful Lord Jesus Christ whom he had served faithfully for so many years as a pastor, teacher and minister. Of himself, Stanley left the following thoughts for us:

"The prize is gained secure
The athlete often fell,
Bore what he could endure,
And bore not always well,
But he may smile at troubles past
Who gains the victor's crown at last.

The lamb is in the fold,
In perfect safety penned:
The lion once had hold
And thought to make an end:
But One with wounded side stood near
And saved his sheep from guilt and fear"

From an ancient hymn

Publisher's Notes

Righteous Books would like express thanks and acknowledgments to the following people:

    To Stanley Voke, in thanks for such opportunities as we have been given and for entrusting us with so much. A friend, a brother, a teacher, whose influence in our lives has been tremendous, challenging us to live more devoted to the Lord Jesus, walking in faith and enjoying his blessing through times of hardship. We miss you dearly, but we look forward to seeing you again one glorious day!

    To Doreen Voke, such an encouragement and a help in our work, a blessing to us all. Thank you for persevering through adversity and helping us through this with editorial advice and opinion, insight and love; for all the prayer and for entrusting the ongoing work to us. We love you!

    To Chris and Peter Voke, for encouragement and research, our sources for Voke family information. And to all of the Voke family for your prayers and blessing in our work with Stanley's ministry.

    To Daniel McCleneghan, "our man in America". For all your support, help, advice, and hard work.

    A big thank you to all of the folks who pray for this work and for the ongoing ministry.

    Thanks also to Pastor Wayne Taylor and Reverend Jim Graham, who have loaned us their names and written our foreword and introduction.

STANLEY VOKE

Walking *HIS WAY*

'...the heart of revival is the moral and spiritual work of the Spirit within us...'

WALKING HIS WAY clearly and concisely addresses the widespread hunger for reality in the Christian life. Stanley Voke's readers will find themselves on the solid ground of God's Word, listening to the Master's voice, bending with the Holy Spirit and realising the kindling of revival in the heart. Revival has been described as 'a new beginning of obedience to God.' This book will do nothing less than bring it within the personal experience of honest seekers.

This is the message of the early church, much neglected, but still essential for those who really want to 'walk His way.'

ISBN 1-900662-00-0
Published by Righteous Books
Now available by direct mail!

Available in the United States from
Living Proof Inc.,
PO Box 637, Bishop, CA 93515

www.righteousbooks.com